# HANDLING LIFE'S

## DISAPPOINTMENTS

Moving from
Desperation to
Celebration

David O. Dykes

First printing, 1993

This book is dedicated to my first love, the Lord Jesus Christ, and to the most wonderful person He has placed in my life—my precious wife, Cindy.

## Also by David O. Dykes

# Contents

# Introduction

*Handling Life's Disappointments* was originally published in 1993. It was not my first published book, but it has remained one of the most popular books I've written. I think that is because everyone experiences disappointment from time to time, and we all need help learning to be victorious despite adversity.

I updated the information in this book for a new release in 2014 and quickly found that God had taught me even more about how to handle the inevitability of life's problems in the past 20 years of ministry than I'd learned in the previous 20 years as a young adult!

## For Further Study

I also included some questions at the end of each chapter to prompt discussion and deepen your understanding of key biblical truths related to the topic at hand. You can use these questions on your own or with a small group. I encourage you to ponder your answers to the questions, study the scriptures, and apply God's truth to your life.

The purpose of this book is to encourage you to learn to rejoice in the midst of your disappointments. I have had to learn these lessons myself, and I am still learning and re-learning many of them as I continue to serve God and walk with Him daily. As I've said many times, suffering is inevitable, but misery is optional. Only through the power of Christ can anyone learn to cope with the myriad of disappointments in life that often result in depression, loneliness, discouragement, and stress. By focusing on Him, the damaging effects of bitterness, low self-esteem, worry, and frustration will be greatly minimized, and you will find true healing from your pain. When you can walk through the valley of some of life's greatest disappointments, and exit rejoicing in the Lord, then you will know that disappointments are really His appointments.

David O. Dykes
September 2014

# CHAPTER 1

# Disappointments Can Be God's Appointments

"Now that I'm a Christian, it means the end of all my problems!" A young single man who had accepted Christ a few days earlier spoke those words to me. There was a flame of enthusiasm burning in his recently transformed heart, but I was afraid he was setting himself up for a major disappointment.

James had recently made the life-changing decision to repent from a lifestyle that was brimming over with problems. His past included drugs, child abuse, and broken relationships. He was currently unemployed and deeply in debt. The thought of a life free of all problems was certainly attractive to him. After all, nearly anything would be an improvement!

I told him that being a Christian did mean the end of his problems—the front end. Since he had accepted Christ, he simply inherited a new and different perspective through which to view his problems. Accepting Christ didn't mean the disappearance of most of his recent problems. He would still face the unpleasant consequences of his bad choices.

"Why would I want to be a Christian then?" he asked with a look of bewilderment furrowing his brow. For the next hour, I talked with James about how Christians are not exempt from painful disappointments and problems. God simply gives us the ability to become "more than conquerors through Him who loved us" (Romans 8:37). In other words, God has given us an "edge" in dealing with disappointments.

The greatest discovery I have made in the Christian life is that God can use times of difficulty and disappointments to reveal His glory to us and through us. I'm convinced that **disappointments can be God's appointments**.

Many Christians stumble over this truth because, like James, they believe that the Christian life will be problem-free. Or they think that minor problems should slide off their lives like an egg on a Teflon-coated pan. They envision the "Teflon-coated" Christian life as:

> All honey; no bees
> No work; all ease

Many sincere Christians are confused because they have listened to a preacher who teaches this belief. Some "televangelist preachers" have concocted a self-satisfying message of health, wealth, and prosperity. They promise that you will enjoy perfect health, abundant wealth, and continued prosperity if you have enough faith. Who can blame thousands of people for listening to that kind of message? Only a fool would choose a life of self-denial and disappointment over a life of full bank accounts and flawless health!

· · · · · · · · · · · · · · · · · · · · · · · · · · · · · · · · · · · · · · · · · · ·

## We can control our mental attitude, and that allows God to meet us in our disappointments.

· · · · · · · · · · · · · · · · · · · · · · · · · · · · · · · · · · · · · · · · · · ·

There is only one flaw in the prosperity-perfection message: it's a lie. When sincere people embrace it and find that they still encounter difficulties, they become self-critical, supposing that their faith must be flawed. Or worse, some may walk away from Christianity, thinking that God can't be trusted to fulfill His promise.

Those who know God intimately have come to see that He often allows us to face adversity in order to conform us to the image of Christ. God determined from the beginning that we should be shaped into the image of His Son. (Romans 8:29) Part of this plan involves the painful removal of those things in our lives that don't reflect this image.

I heard about a man traveling in the Smoky Mountains who stopped at a small, rustic gas station and country store. Outside the store, an elderly man was displaying woodcarvings for sale. He had masterfully created horses, dogs, and other wildlife from blocks of wood. As the visitor examined the art, the old man was busy carving a reproduction of a dog. After watching with fascination he asked the artist, "How do you get such a beautiful image out of a plain block of wood?"

......................................................................

# I'm convinced that disappointments can be God's appointments.

......................................................................

The old man smiled knowingly, having answered that question numerous times. He replied with a twinkle in his eye, "I just cut away everything that doesn't look like a dog!"

## HOW GOD USES DISAPPOINTMENTS

As God is conforming us to be like Jesus, He often uses painful experiences to accomplish His plan. One elderly Quaker got brutally honest with God, as only those who have walked with Him for many years can do. After passing through a series of trials, she prayed, "Lord, I'm surprised you have as many friends as you do ... the way you treat the ones you have!"

Jesus not only promised that we would experience tribulation but also that we could still find sweet victory in the midst of suffering. He said, "In this world you will have trouble. But take heart! I have overcome the world." (John 16:33) While we are not to be of this world, we are still in it, and we can expect disappointments. We have little or no control over many of our circumstances and relationships. However, a victorious Christian is one who recognizes that we can have total control over how we *react* to difficulties. We can control our mental attitude, and that allows God to meet us in our disappointments.

I have received much encouragement from the personal struggles of the apostle Paul. He agonized over a particular problem, which he simply called "a thorn in my flesh." He described it in a letter to some friends:

> To keep me from becoming conceited because of these surpassingly great revelations, there was given me a thorn in my flesh, a messenger of Satan, to torment me. Three times I pleaded with the Lord to take it away from me. But he said to me, "My grace is sufficient for you, for my power is made perfect in weakness." Therefore I will boast all the more gladly about my weaknesses, so that Christ's power may rest on me. That is why, for Christ's sake, I delight in weaknesses, in insults, in hardships, in persecutions, in difficulties. For when I am weak, then I am strong. (2 Corinthians 12:7-10)

Bible scholars will argue for many years about the mystery of this thorn. What was Paul's problem? What was the exact identity of his thorn? The speculations are numerous: eye disease, malaria, epilepsy, a speech impediment, sexual temptation, acute anxiety, pain, a financial bind, and other guesses.

• • • • • • • • • • • • • • • • • • • • • • • • • • • • • • • • • • • • • • • • • • • • • • • • • • • • • • • •

## It may be that God is trying to forge a new character quality in your life through this disappointment.

• • • • • • • • • • • • • • • • • • • • • • • • • • • • • • • • • • • • • • • • • • • • • • • • • • • • • • • •

I chuckle when I read these hypotheses because I tend to think that this thorn is unidentified by design. If we knew the identity of Paul's thorn, we would have trouble identifying with it unless we had the identical problem. Instead, Paul's thorn is like men's socks—one size fits all. You can be certain that whatever the nature of your problem, God's grace is sufficient for you. Paul also described his problem as "the messenger of Satan, to torment me." Indeed, God sometimes allows the devil to affect our lives to make us aware of our need for God's strength. The great preacher A.T. Pierson told of watching a blacksmith working at his trade. With a small hammer, the blacksmith touched the white-hot iron on the anvil and nodded to his helper to hit it as hard as he could with a heavy sledgehammer. Pierson asked, "Why do you first dent it with such tiny taps?" "Oh, I'm just showing him where to hit," was the reply.

## If we knew the identity of Paul's thorn, we would have trouble identifying with it unless we had the identical problem.

Dr. Pierson thought for a moment and then said, "I think we can draw a parable from your actions. Often God puts His finger on the weak points in His servant's life or work and then permits the devil to bring down the sledgehammer blows of affliction to forge him into a stronger man and a better Christian. Thus He makes the devil sweat for the saint's benefit!"

Is there some nagging problem in your life that you can't seem to shake? Paul prayed three times for God to remove his thorn, but He allowed it to remain. Perhaps you have prayed dozens or even hundreds of times for God to relieve you of your difficulty. It may be that God is trying to forge a new character quality in your life through this disappointment.

Don't waste your time asking, "Why, Lord?" Instead, concentrate on asking, "What can I do to give You glory in the midst of this dilemma?" How you react to adversity reveals your character more clearly than how you act in times of peace.

## REVOLT, RESIGN, OR REJOICE?

Christians respond to disappointing difficulties in a variety of ways. Some get angry with God and revolt against Him. They shake their fists toward heaven and complain that they have gotten a raw deal. I'd be a wealthy man if I had a nickel for every time I've heard a Christian whine, "I haven't done anything to deserve this! Why is God mistreating me?" We've all known people who nurse a grudge against God because of some illness, handicap, or difficulty.

........................................................................

# Some people live life on the defensive. They are resigned to suffer and they make sure everyone around them suffers too.

........................................................................

Others cope with their situation with a "que será será" attitude— "what will be, will be." They are simply resigned to the fact that they are going to suffer, so they give up and just accept it. They reflect a martyr complex that lets everyone around them know just how much they are suffering. I heard about a man who missed a step on the stairs going down into his basement. He tumbled down and landed in a painful pile at the bottom. He got up, dusted himself off, and sighed with relief saying, "At least that's over with now!" These people are disciples of the infamous Murphy's Law. Their lives lack joy because they live by the maxim that anything that can go wrong will go wrong. Other variations of this defeated attitude include:

> "Anything you try to fix will take longer and cost more than you think."

> "The chance of a piece of buttered bread falling with the buttered side down is directly proportional to the cost of the

carpet."

"The other line always moves faster."

"When a broken appliance is demonstrated for the repairman, it will always work perfectly."

"Any tool dropped while repairing your car will roll underneath to the exact center."

"No matter how good a bargain you get, you'll always find it somewhere else cheaper after you've bought it."

Some people live life on the defensive. They are resigned to suffer and they make sure everyone around them suffers too. They spend much of their lives preparing to duck the next miserable experience. Some people revolt against suffering; others are simply resigned to it. According to Paul, our reaction to difficulties should instead be one of rejoicing. He said, "Therefore I will boast more gladly about my weaknesses, so that Christ's power may rest on me." (2 Corinthians 12:9)

........................................................

Others cope with their situation with a "que será será" attitude—"what will be, will be." They are simply resigned to the fact that they are going to suffer, so they give up and just accept it.

........................................................

I used to struggle with all of the "rejoice" passages. "Rejoice in the Lord always" (Philippians 4:4); "Be joyful always" (1 Thessalonians 5:16); "Give thanks in all circumstances, for this is God's will for you in Christ Jesus" (1 Thessalonians 5:18). Did that mean I had to rejoice because I broke my leg? I would hear well-meaning believers say, "I thank God for my cancer." "I rejoice that I had this car wreck." I thought they were crazy. Some Christians vainly say, "praise the Lord" simply because they don't cuss. Is this what it means to rejoice in all things?

Notice, Paul didn't thank God for his thorn. Rather, he rejoiced over the power of Christ to cope with and overcome the effects of his problem. He could delight in his disappointments for Christ's sake. God's grace and power became an absolute necessity to him because of his thorn, and that is reason to rejoice!

Chances are, you are going through a time of disappointment right now. You may be struggling with a "thorn," begging God to remove it. If you aren't struggling now, hang on; tribulation is just around the corner. Go ahead and establish in your heart that you are going to face trials as a joyful Christian. Only then are you prepared to deal with the inevitable painful problems of life. Remember, even in the midst of sharp thorns you can often find a beautiful, fragrant rose. I have found this Rose of Sharon to be the sustaining, abiding presence of Jesus Christ.

## TO THINK ABOUT:

- Why do you think some people believe that Christians are exempt from trials?

- Why does God allow us to experience the consequences of our actions even after He has forgiven us?

- Why do you think God wanted Paul to write about his "thorn in the flesh"?

- Is it okay to ask God to remove a certain temptation or problem? What if He chooses not to do so?

- What is your typical response to life's disappointments? Why?

- Think about your last disappointment. Did you revolt against what God was trying to teach you? Did you resign yourself to being a martyr? Or were you able to rejoice in God's grace to carry you through?

- What is the difference between rejoicing about the problem and rejoicing because God can carry you through the problem?

## FOR THE FOLLOWING SCRIPTURES, ASK:

○ What does it say?    ○ What does it mean?    ○ How can you apply it?

- John 16:33
- 2 Corinthians 12:7-10
- 1 Thessalonians 5:18

# CHAPTER 2

# Moving from Desperation to Celebration

Millions of people long every day for just a single word of encouragement. Maybe you are in the middle of the most severe crisis of your life. Or you may have just recently passed through a difficult storm—but chances are that another crisis is just around the bend, waiting to ambush you. Remember, Christians are not exempt from crises. Some people estimate that 1,700 pastors drop out from vocational ministry every month. We label the experience "burnout" or being "stressed out." There are a lot of different terms, but the pain is the same.

Perhaps you awakened one morning, looked in the mirror and came face-to-face with discouragement. You thought, "My life hasn't turned out the way I wanted. I'm not as fulfilled as I thought I would be. I have not accomplished the goals that I thought I would accomplish by this time in my life." Or perhaps you came to a time in your marriage when you no longer felt fulfilled. In many instances, a person simply woke up one day and realized that his or her spouse seemed to be a stranger and wondered how their marriage had deteriorated to that point. Realizations like these have caused a lot of people to drop out of a career or even a marriage. Sometimes they stay put, but the job or the marriage simply leaves them. They just keep going through the motions. The Bible has a lot to say not only about how to survive discouragement but also how to thrive during difficult, discouraging times.

Consider the life of Moses. As Moses led the children of Israel out of Egypt, they encountered the Red Sea. God supernaturally parted the waters and they passed through to the other side. Furthermore, God used the Red Sea to destroy the enemies who were pursuing the Israelites. Yet even after this great spiritual victory, we discover that Moses was not immune to discouragement.

> Then Moses led Israel from the Red Sea and they went into the desert of Shur. For three days they traveled in the desert without finding water. When they came to Marah, they could not drink of its water because it was bitter. That is why the place is called Marah. So the people grumbled against Moses, saying, "What are we to drink?"

> Then Moses cried out to the Lord, and the Lord showed him a piece of wood. He threw it into the water and the water became sweet.

> There the Lord made a decree and a law for them, and there he tested them. He said, "If you listen carefully to the voice of the Lord your God and do what is right in His eyes, if you pay attention to his commands and keep all of his decrees, I will not bring on you any of the diseases I brought on the Egyptians. For I am the Lord who heals you."

> Then they came to Elim, where there were twelve springs and seventy palm trees, and they camped there near the water. (Exodus 15:22-27)

. . . . . . . . . . . . . . . . . . . . . . . . . . . . . . . . . . . . . . . . . . . . . . .

Moses and the children of Israel had just experienced a great spiritual success when God converted an impassable sea into a six-lane superhighway.

. . . . . . . . . . . . . . . . . . . . . . . . . . . . . . . . . . . . . . . . . . . . . . .

## FAILURE AFTER A GREAT SUCCESS

The late Ron Dunn showed me how this passage from Exodus can sweeten the bitter times of discouragement we all encounter. Discouragement is one of the chief tools of the devil. Satan often tempts us with feelings of profound discouragement after we have experienced a great spiritual success. If you are not aware of this principle when you are confronted with discouragement, you may be caught off guard. Why would discouragement strike suddenly when things seem to be going along so smoothly? One moment you are taking a deep breath, and in the next moment, failure and discouragement have a chokehold on you.

............................................................................

Yet even after this great spiritual victory, we discover that Moses was not immune to discouragement.

............................................................................

Moses and the children of Israel had just experienced a great spiritual success when God converted an impassable sea into a six-lane superhighway. After they had crossed safely and their enemies had been eliminated, they took time to celebrate. A song in Exodus 15 is the first recorded in the Bible. They praised God for His deliverance and Moses for his superior leadership. After the party was over, they entered the desert and soon ran out of water. Like spoiled children, the people started criticizing and griping. Their faith in God and Moses vanished.

What was true in the life of Moses occurred in the life of many other biblical characters. After Joshua assumed the leadership role from Moses, he successfully led the children of Israel across the Jordan River. Then they came to Jericho, the most heavily fortified city of the ancient world. It was protected by a series of impregnable walls. However, God had promised that they would capture Jericho without having to shoot a single arrow or hurl a single spear. How could they win? God wanted to deliver the city to them by His power alone. Following God's directions, they marched around

Jericho for seven days. On the seventh day, they walked around it seven times. At a predetermined signal, they shouted and "the walls came tumbling down." Not one Israelite was killed. Wouldn't you call that a great spiritual success?

. . . . . . . . . . . . . . . . . . . . . . . . . . . . . . . . . . . . . . . . . . . . . . . . . . . . . . . . . . . . . . . . . . . . . . . . . .

# What a difference between the pinnacle of Mt. Carmel and the valley under the juniper tree.

. . . . . . . . . . . . . . . . . . . . . . . . . . . . . . . . . . . . . . . . . . . . . . . . . . . . . . . . . . . . . . . . . . . . . . . . . .

But do you recall what happened immediately after that? A group of soldiers decided to go down to a one-horse town named Ai. In the ensuing battle against this tiny village, 36 Israelites were killed. The remaining soldiers went running back to Joshua in shame and defeat. They conquered mighty Jericho, but they were defeated by little Ai? It turned out that the secret sin of a man named Achan was responsible for their failure. Sometimes it's our personal sin that will often cause failure after a great success.

Consider another example. The Bible tells us that Elijah was a prophet of God who had the courage to challenge the evil prophets of Baal. One day he ascended Mt. Carmel and stood alone against 450 false prophets. He challenged the people by saying, "How long will you waver between two opinions? If the Lord is God, follow him; but if Baal is God, follow him … you call on the name of your god, and I will call upon the name of the Lord. The god who answers by fire—he is God." (1 Kings 18:21, 24)

For much of the day, the prophets of Baal prayed for their god to send down fire. They prayed, danced, and mutilated their bodies to no avail. Toward the end of the day, Elijah had endured their frantic activity long enough. After having his sacrifice soaked in water, he prayed a simple prayer, and God answered with fire. What a tremendous spiritual victory! But what happened immediately afterward? In the next scene, Elijah was sitting under a tree having a

pity party, wanting to die. What a difference between the pinnacle of
Mt. Carmel and the valley under the juniper tree.

> # If you are prepared to face discouragement after a great spiritual success, you can deal with it according to God's power.

This pattern of defeat after victory continued into the New
Testament. Someone has said that the only time Peter ever opened
his mouth was to change feet! Although he seldom said the right
thing in the right way, there was at least one instance when he
responded correctly. In Matthew 16, Jesus asked the disciples about
His identity. Only Peter correctly identified and proclaimed Jesus as
the Son of God. I can just imagine Peter puffing up with pride after
Jesus praised him, but the gray matter between his ears didn't reveal
that truth to Peter; rather, God revealed it directly to him. However,
later in the same chapter of Matthew, Jesus gathered His disciples
and revealed to them that He was going to Jerusalem to die. Peter,
who was certainly still enjoying the status of being a recipient of
divine revelation, interrupted Jesus and challenged His plan.

> Peter took Jesus aside and began to rebuke him. "Never, Lord!" he said.
> "This shall never happen to you!"

> Jesus turned and said to Peter, "Get behind me, Satan! You are a stumbling
> block to me; you do not have in mind the things of God, but the things of
> men." (Matthew 16:22-23)

Earlier, Peter was a channel of divine revelation; now he was
a channel of devilish recrimination. If you do not recognize this
pattern of spiritual defeat after victory, discouragement will ambush

you from out of nowhere. However, if you are prepared to face discouragement after a great spiritual success, you can deal with it according to God's power.

Don't think that you have necessarily missed God's will if you find yourself discouraged. God led Moses and the children of Israel to the bitter water of Marah. It was all part of His plan. God did not test them at the Red Sea. Rather, He tested them at Marah. We must realize that God doesn't usually test us during times of great spiritual victory, but during episodes of spiritual stress. He is interested to see how we react when we face challenging circumstances and perplexing people.

In the case of Moses' discouragement, it stemmed from the criticism he faced after the water at Marah proved bitter. Water is a basic necessity of life, but we usually take it for granted. We don't even notice water until we don't have it or it becomes distasteful. Like water, there may be some basic realities of your life that you have taken for granted. These basic relationships and experiences go unnoticed until they become bitter; then we notice them in a hurry!

It may be that your marriage is at Marah. Like cool water, your marriage should refresh and strengthen you. Have you taken your marriage for granted? Only when you face difficulties do you notice that there is a problem. Has your relationship with your spouse become tasteless? I've known many people who are at Marah in their marriage. They complain with distaste about the bitterness of a stale relationship.

## Perhaps you are still singing in the choir, but you no longer enjoy it. It has become bitter.

You may be at Marah in your vocation. Your job should nourish and delight you. You should wake up in the morning looking forward to going to work and accomplishing something. Sadly, for millions of Americans, work is bitter and tasteless. Has your job become nothing more than a boring daily routine?

You may be at Marah in your service for the Lord. Perhaps you are still singing in the choir, but you no longer enjoy it. It has become bitter. You may be teaching Sunday school, but you are doing it just because someone has to do it. There is no joy, no sweetness. You know you should receive great joy from that service, but a bitter aftertaste is all that you have.

........................................................................

You may be tempted to quit on your marriage, your job, your Christian service, your personal walk with the Lord, or your relationship with those around you.

........................................................................

Committed Christians can even come to Marah in their personal devotional life. It may be that you are still maintaining a quiet time with the Lord, but it has deteriorated into a mere routine. It is just something that you do because you know that you should do it. You may be at Marah in terms of relationships with loved ones. Are you struggling with the bitterness of a rebellious child or caring for elderly parents? Maybe you have a relative who is causing you great heartache. Relationships should bless us like a cool drink of water on a hot day, but they can become as bitter as Marah.

Discouragement whispers in our ear: "Just quit." Several times Moses was tempted to give up on the Israelites. You may be tempted to quit on your marriage, your job, your Christian service, your personal walk with the Lord, or your relationship with those around you. Quitting is the easy thing to do. Endurance requires the power of God.

## CRITICIZED AFTER WE SERVE OTHERS

Moses had done his best to follow God, and yet the very people he helped deliver from bondage were now criticizing him. You must realize that you will often be criticized even though you are doing your best. Prepare to be unappreciated. After Moses led the people across the Red Sea, he was their hero. A few miles farther down the road, he became a zero! He who had been the object of their adoration became the target of their condemnation. At the Red Sea they sang his praises; at Marah they challenged his wisdom.

How should you respond when you do your best and others condemn you? First of all, when you are criticized, don't take it personally. Moses was simply obeying God. If you are following God to the best of your ability, don't take it personally when you become a target for the poisonous arrows of criticism. If you displease God, it doesn't matter whom you please; however, if you please God, it doesn't matter whom you displease.

> If you are following God to the best of your ability, don't take it personally when you become a target for the poisonous arrows of criticism.

Moses gives us a second suggestion on how to deal with criticism. Don't take it out on those you love. Criticism and grumbling can become contagious. When we are criticized, our natural reflex is to look around for someone else to criticize. This "scapegoat syndrome" is where the boss hollers at the husband, the husband goes home and hollers at his wife, she in turn hollers at the teenager, the teenager hollers at the child, the child goes out and kicks the dog, the dog chases the cat, and the poor cat asks, "What did I do?" If we are not careful, a vicious cycle of criticism can develop. When you are the target of criticism, don't pass it on; let it die.

················································································

# When you are the target of criticism, don't pass it on; let it die.

················································································

The people who criticized Moses at Marah were not finished complaining. Later Moses refused the opportunity to take revenge against them when they complained again after arriving at Kadesh-Barnea. God instructed them to proceed into the Promised Land, but some were not so sure about that. (Someone has said that it must have been a Baptist congregation because the first thing they did was elect a committee to check it out!) The 12 spies returned, but 10 of them gave a majority report that said the land was unconquerable. Only Joshua and Caleb proclaimed that with the strength of God, the land could be taken. Moses gathered the people to make a decision, but the people voted in favor of staying out of the Promised Land. God had commanded them to enter, but they disobeyed.

> The Lord said to Moses, "How long will these people treat me with contempt? How long will they refuse to believe in me, in spite of all the miraculous signs I have performed among them? I will strike them down with a plague and destroy them, but I will make you into a nation greater and stronger than they." (Numbers 14:11-12)

God was so angry that He planned to destroy the people and take Moses' family to conquer the land. If Moses had harbored resentment and anger toward those who were criticizing him, he would have quickly agreed to this plan. If he had chosen to do so, it is possible that in centuries to come people would not have talked so much about Abraham and his family, but of Moses and *his* family. Amazingly, Moses declined God's offer to destroy his rebellious followers. Instead, he pleaded with God on behalf of these difficult, critical people. He prayed, "In accordance with your great love, forgive the sin of these people, just as you have pardoned them from the time they left Egypt until now." (Numbers 14:19)

.....................................................................................

# Instead of focusing on your discouraging situation, focus upon the cross.

.....................................................................................

Moses demonstrated Christ-like humility. After all, how did Jesus respond to criticism? "When they hurled their insults at him, he did not retaliate; when he suffered he made no threats. Instead, he entrusted himself to him who judges justly." (1 Peter 2:23) Several years ago, a good friend gave me a framed parchment that contained words attributed to Theodore Roosevelt. I have often read this quote and received encouragement in the face of discouraging criticism:

> It is not the critic who counts, not the one who points out how the strong man stumbled or how the doer of deeds might have done them better. The credit belongs to the man who is actually in the arena, whose face is marred with sweat and dust, and blood; who strives valiantly; who errs and comes short again and again; who knows the great enthusiasm, the great devotions, and spends himself in a worthy cause; who, if he wins, knows the triumphant of high achievement; and who, if he fails, at least fails while daring greatly, so that his place shall never be with those cold and timid souls who know neither victory nor defeat.

How then should we respond when we are criticized? Don't take it personally, and don't take it out on those you love. Instead, take it to the Lord. That's what Moses did. He cried out to the Lord and the Lord provided a simple solution. I have found that during the most discouraging times of my life, I am driven to my knees in fervent prayer. God allows us to go through periods of discouragement so that we can be tested and tried. One of the ways we pass the test is by simply drawing closer to Him in prayer.

Have you tried turning to God in the face of your bitter discouragement? Have you cried out to God about your dissatisfying marriage, job, or your Christian service? God is the only One who can change your bitterness into sweetness.At Marah, God instructed Moses to take an ordinary tree and put it in the bitter water.

········································································

# When we are at a discouraging point in our lives, we are tempted to sit down and quit.

········································································

Through that simple act, the water became sweet. I am immediately reminded of the "tree" in the New Testament—that is, the tree upon which our Lord Jesus was crucified. It has been a great source of help for me to immerse the cross in my bitter situation. Only then do I find the sweetness of the "power of the sufferings" of Jesus Christ that Paul talks about in Philippians 3:10. Instead of focusing on your discouraging situation, focus upon the cross. Immerse the cross in your discouragement and allow God to sweeten your soul.

## REFRESHMENT AFTER GREAT SUFFERING

After the difficulty of Marah, Moses and the people came to a paradise named Elim (Exodus 15:27). Marah represents discouragement and bitterness. Elim represents a surplus of fullness and refreshment because they found 12 wells of water and 70 palm trees there. The question we face is this: How can I move from Marah to Elim? How can I get from bitterness to fullness in my marriage, job, personal walk with the Lord, or in my relationships? How can I change my focus from desperation to celebration?

To get from Marah to Elim, you simply endure and don't quit. A

quick survey of a biblical map reveals that Elim is only five miles from
Marah. What a tragedy it would have been if the Israelites had quit
at Marah! When we are at a discouraging point in our lives, we are
tempted to sit down and quit. But Elim is just down the road. When
you are at a bitter time in your marriage, don't call the divorce lawyer;
Elim is just down the road. If you're at a discouraging point in your
job, think twice before you walk out. Elim could be closer than you
think. If you are tempted to give up on a certain relationship or resign
from serving the Lord, don't do it! You can usually discover a wave of
refreshment if you will just keep on going despite the pain.

## Discouragement says, "I quit!" Endurance says, "I will not give up yet."

There is much to be said about the benefit of simple, old-
fashioned endurance. Our world glamorizes quitting in movies
and commercials, and we dream of doing the same one day.
Discouragement says, "I quit!" Endurance says, "I will not give up
yet." As you review the last 10 years of your life, is there anything
that you now wish that you had not quit? The problem for most of
us is that we simply quit too soon. Elim, with its tranquility and
refreshment, is just down the road.

I have a friend who is a pastor in Alaska. When he was driving
with his family up to Anchorage, they traveled on the Alcan
Highway. They had sold most of their possessions in Texas and put
what was left in a trailer they pulled behind their car. The Alcan
Highway is a primitive road that is often unpaved because of the
damage that freezing temperatures can do to pavement. The AlCan
snakes its way through some of the most barren, beautiful wilderness
on the globe. As they were driving late one afternoon, they were
startled to see a large bear cross the highway right in front of their

car. It was the first bear they had seen, and it scared them to death.

To make matters worse, my friend noticed at that moment that his gas tank was dangerously near empty. The gas stations and restaurants are sparsely scattered along the highway with many miles between. As he drove away, with the bear in his rearview mirror, he became progressively fearful they would soon run out of gas. Just as darkness settled, with no gas station in sight, he decided to park beside the road rather than risk running totally out of gas. They huddled together, hoping another vehicle would come along and help them, but no traffic passed during the entire night. They were so afraid that the bear might still be in their vicinity that they never got out of the car. The five of them tossed and turned in the crowded, cold car all night and slept very little.

························································

# The greatest days of your marriage, your job, your Christian service, and your relationships may be in front of you. Don't stop yet.

························································

The next morning when the sun arose, he started his car, asking God to help them find another traveler or a gas station soon. As he crested the top of a ridge, he saw a gas station, restaurant, and 24-hour motel at the bottom of the hill! They had spent a miserable night less than a mile from gas, hot food, and a warm bed because they stopped a little too soon!

The greatest days of your marriage, your job, your Christian service, and your relationships may be in front of you. Don't stop yet. There will be failures; you can be sure. You can count on being criticized. But remember, learning to endure despite any discouragement will allow you to move from desperation to celebration.

## TO THINK ABOUT:

- In what area of your life do you currently feel unfulfilled? Explain.

- Why is discouragement one of the "chief tools" of the devil?

- When was a time you experienced a spiritual challenge right after a great victory? What did you learn from that experience?

- How do you usually respond to criticism?

- When are you tempted to quit too soon? What action steps can you take to learn to persevere when times get tough?

- What is the value of endurance?

## FOR THE FOLLOWING SCRIPTURES, ASK:

○ What does it say?   ○ What does it mean?   ○ How can you apply it?

- John 15:18
- James 1:4
- 1 Peter 2:23

# CHAPTER 3

# When You've Got the "Blahs"

What do great men such as Abraham Lincoln, Albert Schweitzer, Winston Churchill, and Charles Spurgeon have in common? A careful study of their biographies reveals that all of these men struggled with depression. Spurgeon, the London pastor who preached to over 5,000 people each Sunday, often found himself in such depths of depression that he had to take frequent retreats out of town. At age 43, he made 20 fall-winter trips to the south of France. Depression drove him from his pulpit for much of the year, but his church said, "We would rather have you one month in the year than any other preacher for twelve."[1]

Depression is no less a problem today. One in four adults—approximately 61.5 million Americans—experiences mental illness in a given year. One in 17—about 13.6 million—lives with a serious mental illness such as schizophrenia, major depression, or bipolar disorder.[2]

Studies reveal that women are twice as likely to be treated for depression; however, men are four or five times more likely to commit suicide. In general, women more easily admit their depression and seek therapy for it, while men tend to be out of touch with their feelings of emptiness. Men struggle to adequately

---

1   Richard Ellsworth Day, *The Shadow of the Broad Brim.* (Philadelphia: Judson Press, 1934), p. 175.
2   National Institutes of Health, National Institute of Mental Health, http://www.nami.org/factsheets/mentalillness_factsheet.pdf, accessed September 1, 2014.

express their depression. As men, we are trained to deny our feelings and to take action instead. We try to act tough and manly, no matter how we are really feeling.

If you are suffering from the "blahs," you need to distinguish between clinical depression and temporary seasons of depressing thoughts. Most people pass through times of depression, but clinical depression can be damaging to your health. Depression is not just sadness; it is a state of mind that makes it difficult for people to envision that their lives, or anything they do, will turn out well.[3] A depressed person feels life is hopeless and there is no solution in sight.

## UNDERSTANDING DEPRESSION

It is important to recognize the differences between depression and other emotional problems. For instance, depression should not be confused with grief. When one experiences the loss of someone or something precious, that person passes through the process of grief. This grieving process is healthy and normal. Grief is not depression; however, if grief is not resolved, it can deteriorate into long-term, dangerous depression.

> A depressed person feels life is hopeless and there is no solution in sight.

Don't confuse depression with guilt either. When a person sins or commits a shameful act, he or she experiences nagging guilt. This guilt is not depression—a feeling of guilt is normal as it relates

---

3    Frank Pittman, MD, "A Cry For Help," *New Woman Magazine*, September 1991, p. 132.

to sinful behavior. Our God-given conscience causes us to feel remorse and pain over sin. For a Christian, forgiveness from guilt can be found in Jesus Christ. When we confess our sins, our guilt is replaced by a sense of gratitude for God's forgiveness. So be careful that you don't confuse other negative emotions with depression. Most experts tell us that depression is caused by a combination of physical, emotional, and mental factors. They have identified four basic types of depression:

1. **Endogenous depression** is caused by a chemical imbalance in the central nervous system. Many people are relieved to discover that there may be a purely physical reason for their depression. A person suffering from diabetes, hypoglycemia, or other medical problems may experience depression because of an imbalance of chemicals in his system. When a person describes feelings of depression, I generally encourage him to see a medical doctor and undergo a complete physical. This is one reason why alcohol is especially dangerous for depression. It triggers a brutal chemical assault on the brain. Alcohol may offer a brief escape from the pain, but it will ultimately deepen the agony.

2. **Reactive depression** is a response to severe personal disappointment. It may be caused by divorce, loss of job, or loss of health. Some traumatic event causes the victim to fall into a period of depression.

3. **Toxic depression** is caused by the influence of outside substances on the nervous system. Alcohol, drugs, diet, or a virus may lead to toxic depression. When the damaging substance is removed, the depression leaves.

4. **Psychotic depression** is caused by a combination of factors, which often lead to a nervous breakdown or burnout.[4]

---

4   Nelson Price, *Farewell to Fear*. (Nashville: Broadman Press, 1983), p. 110.

Depression is a feeling of despair and sadness that communicates to a person that his life is out of control. A depressed person not only feels that there is no immediate help but also that there is no future hope. You are depressed when you cannot see "the light at the end of the tunnel." You can't even find the tunnel! One person said, "I knew I was in trouble when I saw that 'the light at the end of the tunnel' was an approaching train!"

········································································

# If you or someone you know is suffering from depression, there is hope and help in God's Word.

········································································

You may be asking yourself, "How can I tell if I'm clinically depressed?" Dr. Wayne Oates has summarized the symptoms of clinical depression. Dr. Oates, who taught in the Psychiatric Department of the University of Louisville Medical School, has listed ten symptoms of depression.[5] If you answer yes to five or more of these questions, you may be suffering from clinical depression.

1.  Have you suddenly or slowly lost all initiative toward other people?

2.  Do you exercise repeated crying spells that have no apparent cause?

3.  Have you persistently over a period of weeks awakened suddenly and been unable to return to sleep for more than half an hour?

4.  Do you awaken in the morning feeling fatigued and face the day with dread?

5   From author's class notes, Southern Baptist Theological Seminary, Louisville, Kentucky, 1975.

5. Do you feel pain of "scattered, unspecific kind, aching all over"?

6. Do you find yourself thinking about your own death, wishing life were over or that you are afraid you might commit suicide?

7. Do you breathe irregularly, sigh repeatedly, and feel "heavy in the chest"?

8. Do you distrust your own wisdom, have unusual trouble making decisions, and feel generally helpless?

9. Do you find yourself irritable, cross, without cause?

10. Do you have great trouble being enthusiastic about anything?

---

# A depressed person not only feels that there is no immediate help but also that there is no future hope.

---

While we all suffer periods of depressing thoughts, we should be on guard against sinking into clinical depression. If you are suicidal or suspect you are clinically depressed, please seek professional help from a counselor and/or your physician. If you or someone you know is suffering from depression, there is hope and help in God's Word.

## IDENTIFYING THE CAUSES OF DEPRESSION

People often express the desire to be like Bible characters because they believe they were free from pain and difficulties. Nothing could be further from the truth. We can learn much about depression by studying the life of Elijah, a prophet who suffered from it. In 1 Kings 19:1-9, we see Elijah sitting under a juniper tree praying in despair and telling God he'd had all he could take. He wanted God to take away his life because it wasn't worth living anymore. Does that sound familiar? Have you ever confessed to God that you have had more than you can take?

Before we can understand the causes of depression, we must realize that God created us as a body, a soul, and a spirit. (1 Thessalonians 5:23) Therefore, depression may arise from a physical problem (body), an emotional problem (soul), a spiritual problem (spirit), or a combination of any of these.

### Physical Symptoms

First, we are most vulnerable to depression when we are physically drained. When you become tired and run down, you are a prime candidate for depression. Do you remember what happened to Elijah before he found himself in the depths of despair? He had recently experienced a stressful confrontation on Mt. Carmel where he boldly challenged the prophets of Baal. He was victorious when God delivered a spectacular firestorm from heaven and allowed him to dispose of all the false prophets. However, the vicious death threats of Jezebel soon sent him running for his life for over 30 miles to Beersheba. It is obvious that he had lost sleep, neglected his diet, and was at the breaking point physically. No wonder he was depressed!

......................................................................

## He was victorious when God delivered a spectacular firestorm from heaven and allowed him to dispose of all the false prophets.

......................................................................

Good health is preventive medicine against depression, and physical fitness is a very effective therapy if you become depressed.

Our bodies can take only so much abuse, and if we keep our physical tachometer pegged in the red, we will soon pay the price.

Do you recall watching those old television shows with a person spinning plates on top of poles? He would spin a plate on top of a pole, run to the next pole, spin a plate on top of it, and then run and do the same with another. He would do this until he had 40 plates spinning at one time. Then he would run from pole to pole and spin the plates to keep them going. That describes the lifestyle of many Americans. Many of us have so many plates spinning that we spend our lives running from one project to another, trying to maintain balance. We simply cannot function at breakneck speed, 24 hours per day. When our bodies get tired, we are susceptible to depression.

· · · · · · · · · · · · · · · · · · · · · · · · · · · · · · · · · · · · · · · · · · · · · · · · ·

## Many of us have so many plates spinning that we spend our lives running from one project to another, trying to maintain balance.

· · · · · · · · · · · · · · · · · · · · · · · · · · · · · · · · · · · · · · · · · · · · · · · · ·

Vince Lombardi was a great football coach, not only because he understood football but also because he understood people. He once said, "Fatigue makes cowards of us all." It is common among depressed people to suffer from a lack of adequate rest. Are you suffering from "sleep deficit"? Physicians tell us that our bodies were not designed to survive on four or five hours of sleep per night. You may function for a short period of time with very little sleep, but you will accumulate a sleep deficit that gets deeper and deeper until it catches up to you. The penalty is usually some form of emotional or mental problem.

### Emotional Symptoms

Second, we are vulnerable to depression when we are emotionally depleted. Not only was Elijah physically tired, but also he was emotionally rung out. He had been dealing with difficult people. Jezebel and her husband Ahab were threatening him. If you are not careful, people will drain you emotionally. Someone has said, "You don't have to be a cannibal to be fed up with people!" Emotional problems are most often caused by relational problems. We may suffer an onset of depression when we are having problems with our spouse, children, neighbor, or business associate. Take a moment to identify any relational problems with which you are struggling.

Some people claim that suicidal urges always accompany depression. That is not always so. Was Elijah actually suicidal? I don't think so. If he really wanted to die, all he had to do was stop running. Jezebel would have taken care of that problem for him! No, he was simply burned out emotionally from dealing with difficult people. Has that happened to you?

### Spiritual Symptoms

Third, we also get depressed when we are spiritually defeated. In addition to Elijah's physical and emotional problem, he suffered from a spiritual issue. He sat under that tree drinking deeply of the intoxicating cup of self-pity. He had recently concluded a great spiritual endeavor, and now he was waiting for someone to pat him on the back. He stuck out his bottom lip at God and complained that he was the "only one" left who was faithful.

..................................................................................

# Consider the physical, emotional, and spiritual causes for depression. Which source is affecting you?

..................................................................................

We can be guilty of the same mistake. After we have experienced a great spiritual high, we often become self-satisfied and complacent. In pride, we may think that we are the only one still being truly faithful to God. This attitude leads to spiritual paranoia where we constantly compare ourselves to others. We need to be sure that we aren't like the man who refused to attend a football game because he was convinced that when the team went into a huddle they were talking about him!

Consider the physical, emotional, and spiritual causes for depression. Which source is affecting you? Here is a quick self-test to determine your depression level. Imagine that there are three gauges on the dashboard of your personality—a physical gauge, an emotional gauge, and a spiritual gauge. On the left side of each gauge there is an "E" for empty, and on the right side an "F" for full. If you drew those three gauges on a sheet of paper and registered your present condition, how would you measure up? Are you empty physically, emotionally, or spiritually? Where is your needle pointing? Before you can deal with your depression, you must identify the areas of emptiness in your life.

## OVERCOMING DEPRESSION

Sometimes Christians experience guilt for feeling depressed. They feel that they should "have it all together." But even committed believers struggle with depression. The good news is that a believer can discover that there is hope from God. Though you may be walking through the valley of depression, it is possible for you to walk *out* of that valley. While in that dark valley, you can discover that indeed Jesus is the Lily of the Valley (Song of Solomon 2:1). How can you overcome your depression?

................................................................

Though you may be walking through the valley of depression, it is possible for you to walk *out* of that valley.

................................................................

First, if your problem is basically physical, strengthen your body. There is no quick fix for depression. You did not get into your depressed state overnight; neither will you get out of it in such a short span. In our "microwave society," people are always looking for a quick fix. They want a pill to take, a book to read, or an app to download that will immediately relieve their depression.

Instead, if you are in a depressed state, think of yourself as a battery that needs recharging. When I was a young man working at a gas station, a car battery could be charged one of two ways. A mechanic could put a "quick charge" into the battery by infusing a massive shock for about 15 minutes. This would recharge the battery, but it sometimes damaged it. However, there was another more effective method called a "trickle charge." Over a period of several hours, the mechanic gradually introduced a small amount of power until the battery was completely recharged.

While most of us are looking for a "quick charge," God wants to renew us through a slower process. That's how he restored Elijah. First, God was careful to see that He helped Elijah recharge physically. Elijah was too proud to admit that he was tired, so God simply placed him into a deep sleep. Then God sent a "chef angel" to feed him. Elijah awakened to find a warm cake and cool water. (Could this be "angel food cake"? I wonder!) Then God put Elijah back to sleep and repeated this process. He provided even more sleep and more food. Elijah had been neglecting his diet and rest. Have you overlooked the importance of those two things?

> There is no quick fix for depression. You did not get into your depressed state overnight.

Next, God accompanied Elijah on a steady hike for the next forty days. (1 Kings 19:8) This journey provided exercise, which is essential to reducing the potential for depression. We can learn from Elijah's experience that it is important for us to eat correctly, to get plenty of rest, and to exercise our bodies. Health care professionals tell us that there is a direct correlation between physical health and mental wellbeing. For many people, a conscientious program of physical fitness is the first step out of depression.

### Help from Others

Perhaps you are already physically fit. If your problem is basically emotional or relational, you should share your burden with someone else. When God started bringing Elijah out of his depression, He revealed to him that there were many other people with whom Elijah could network. God told him that there were actually 7,000 other people in Israel who had not bowed their knees to Baal. God instructed Elijah to find an assistant, Elisha, to help him with his work. By sharing his burden, Elijah found relief from depression (verses 18-19).

........................................................................

## For many people, a conscientious program of physical fitness is the first step out of depression.

........................................................................

In the same way, it is important for you to share your burden with other people. This may mean simply sharing with someone close to you that you are feeling miserable and suffering from depression. Admitting the problem is the first step to finding relief. Can you think of someone you can trust, like a counselor, a friend, or a spouse to share your innermost thoughts and concerns? As Christians, we are to "carry each other's burdens." (Galatians 6:2)

Have you ever taken a relational inventory? Try writing down the names of the people with whom you interact. As you consider these names, you will discover that most of them fall into three categories. First, there are some people who drain you emotionally. They cause your emotional gauge to slide from full to empty. They are always demanding, and you feel that you are always giving to them. Second, there are some people who could be categorized as simply neutral. You may like them, and they don't drain you emotionally. Third, there are some people you may identify who are replenishing. These are people whom you love, and when you are with them, they make your emotional needle surge from empty to full. They encourage and support you.

**If your depression is caused by a spiritual problem, you can survey your blessings.**

Now that you know where the people in your life fall in a relational inventory, what can you do about it? If possible, make an intentional effort to limit the time you spend with those who drain you. Also, try to improve your relationship with those who are "neutral" so that they may become replenishing to you. The best way to do this is to be a replenishing kind of person to others. Third, make sure that you spend plenty of time with those friends and family members who refresh and replenish you.

### Spiritual Help

If your depression is caused by a spiritual problem, you can survey your blessings. That was another strategy God used to draw Elijah out of his depression. God took Elijah to a mountain in Horeb. He then amazed Elijah with a divine demonstration of lightning, rain, thunder, and earthquakes. Elijah was looking for God, but he didn't find Him in that dramatic event. Instead, God spoke to him in a whisper. He reassured him that He was still in control. Then God outlined the next step Elijah should take. He comforted Elijah and told him that things were not as bad as he thought. I imagine that Elijah then looked around and started seeing how good things really were. Spending this extended time alone with God changed Elijah's state of being.

When was the last time you got alone with God and listened for the same still, small voice Elijah heard? Christians often find themselves in a depression when they neglect their quiet time. God used the thunder, lightning, and earthquakes simply to get Elijah's attention. Could it be that God is using some crisis in your life to get you to focus on Him? Open your eyes and look around to see what God is really trying to say to you.

## NOTHING IS HOPELESS

If you are still depressed even though these other areas of your life are "in check," you may also need help in the form of medication that can be prescribed by a medical professional when the cause of your depression is caused by a chemical imbalance. The chemicals you need to maintain a particular area of the brain may not be sufficient, and medication can address this deficiency. I know Christians who feel they are somehow "weak" in their faith if they resort to medication to help them with depression. However, would you say you are weak if you wore a cast on a broken arm? Certainly not. Sometimes our bodies and brains need help, and we are wise to seek professional help when other means of dealing with depression are not enough.

............................................................

Could it be that God is using some crisis in your life to get you to focus on Him?

............................................................

Even in depression, a Christian should never say that it is hopeless. The words to a hymn called *Count Your Blessings*, say, "When upon life's billows you are tempest tossed/when you are discouraged thinking all is lost/count your many blessings, name them one by one/ and it will surprise you what the Lord has done." With God, there is help for today and hope for tomorrow. I love the story about a little boy who was in a pet store to choose a new puppy. As he looked down into the pen, he saw a number of puppies running and jumping around. There was one particularly frisky puppy whose tail was wagging furiously. The little boy smiled and said, "I want the one with the happy ending!"

· · · · · · · · · · · · · · · · · · · · · · · · · · · · · · · · · · · · · · · · · · · · · ·

## Take positive steps to walk out of the valley, holding the hand of the Savior.

· · · · · · · · · · · · · · · · · · · · · · · · · · · · · · · · · · · · · · · · · · · · · ·

As a Christian, we have the promise of hope. With Christ, our lives are guaranteed to have happy endings when we are in heaven with Him one day. And with Christ, we are guaranteed that His power and His presence will sustain us in times of difficulty. As you examine your life, determine whether or not you are suffering from clinical depression. If so, seek professional help. However, if you are going through seasons of depression, examine yourself physically, emotionally, and spiritually. Take positive steps to walk out of the valley, holding the hand of the Savior.

## TO THINK ABOUT

- Why do you think so many people struggle with depression?

- This chapter mentions physical, emotional, and spiritual symptoms of depression. In which of the three areas are you most vulnerable? Why?

- What action steps can you take to strengthen yourself physically to guard against depression?

- Are you more likely to help others carry their burdens or to share your burdens with others?

- How can you remind yourself more often of your blessings? How do you cultivate gratefulness?

- Why do Christians always have hope?


## FOR THE FOLLOWING SCRIPTURES, ASK:
○ What does it say?    ○ What does it mean?    ○ How can you apply it?

- Psalm 130:5-7
- Galatians 6:2
- 1 Thessalonians 5:23

# CHAPTER 4

# A Remedy for Loneliness

Woven into the very fabric of our American culture is a dark thread of loneliness. Many people of my generation will remember the rock singer, Janis Joplin. Joplin would strut onto stage with a microphone in one hand and a bottle of Southern Comfort bourbon in the other as she electrified the crowd with her animated performance. At the height of her career, she was making over $2 million a year. Joplin possessed money, fame, and popularity. She was surrounded by people who wanted to be her friend. Her future seemed to be bright.

In spite of her success, one night after a concert she returned to her apartment in Los Angeles and injected a lethal overdose of heroin into her veins. On the night of her suicide, the reports said she had commented to one of her friends about her utter loneliness and how she just stared at the television whenever she was not on stage.[6] A generation earlier, Marilyn Monroe had swallowed an overdose of sleeping pills. Although she was in the spotlight, she also expressed feelings of intense loneliness. In 2014, Robin Williams— one of the zaniest comedians to ever hit the big screen—shocked the world by taking his own life. Celebrities are only representative of the millions of people who suffer from loneliness.

Music is usually a reflection of the values and problems of a specific culture. If you listen carefully, you will find the theme of loneliness

---

6    Adrian Rogers, *Mastering Your Emotions* (Nashville, Tennesee: Broadman Press, 1988), p. 99.

running through much of our music. Older songs like "Only The Lonely" and "Mr. Lonely" are indicative of our widespread loneliness. Hank Williams sang about being so lonesome he thought he might die. Elvis Presley touched a sensitive nerve in the hearts of many people when he asked the question, "Are you lonesome tonight?" The fabulous four from Liverpool, the Beatles, sang about "all the lonely people."

When we think of a lonely person, we usually picture a poor little widow who lives all alone. I've known widows who weren't lonely at all; while at the same time I've seen divorced or married people cleverly conceal their loneliness. It is possible to be surrounded by many people, with hundreds of "friends" on Facebook, and still be oppressively lonely. You may be married, have a family, and have many people who consider you to be their friend and still suffer from loneliness. Even President Jimmy Carter spoke of the "loneliness of the Presidency."

. . . . . . . . . . . . . . . . . . . . . . . . . . . . . . . . . . . . . . . . . . . . . . . . . . . . . . . . . . . .

## When we think of a lonely person, we usually picture a poor little widow who lives all alone.

. . . . . . . . . . . . . . . . . . . . . . . . . . . . . . . . . . . . . . . . . . . . . . . . . . . . . . . . . . . .

Because the Bible speaks to every variety of human emotions, it has a lot to say about loneliness. The Old Testament character Job experienced overwhelming tragedy, sorrow, and loneliness. He cried out in anguish to God:

> He has alienated my brothers from me; my acquaintances are completely estranged from me. My kinsmen have gone away; my friends have forgotten me. My guests and my maidservants count me a stranger; they look upon me as an alien. I summon my servant, but he does not answer, though I beg him with my own mouth. My breath is offensive to my wife; I am loathsome to my own brothers. Even the little boys scorn me; when I appear, they ridicule me. All my intimate friends detest me; those I love have turned against me. (Job 19:13-19)

Family, friends, and servants surrounded Job, but he suffered from a sense of alienation. His predicament grew so intense that it is almost comical. His servants didn't respond when he called. His guests looked at him without recognizing his identity. His wife nagged him about his bad breath. Even preschool boys were mocking him! He felt that his closest friends were now his enemies, plotting against him. Have you ever possessed feelings similar to Job? Have you ever felt that the people closest to you really were isolated from you? Even the godliest characters in the Bible like Job suffered from loneliness. Today many committed Christians can't seem to shake the curse of bitter loneliness.

......................................................................

# It is possible to be surrounded by many people, with hundreds of "friends" on Facebook, and still be oppressively lonely.

......................................................................

Medical doctors have written much in recent years of the tragic consequences of loneliness. Between 1985 and 2004, the number of people who said there was no one with whom they discussed important matters tripled, to 25 percent, according to Duke University researchers.[7]

How lonely you feel today actually predicts how well you'll sleep tonight and how depressed you'll feel a year from now, according to John T. Cacioppo, a neuroscientist at the University of Chicago and coauthor of *Loneliness: Human Nature and the Need for Social Connection*.[8]

---

7   http://www.newsweek.com/lonely-planet-isolation-increases-us-78647, accessed August 13, 2014.
8   Ibid.

## ARE YOU SUFFERING FROM LONELINESS?

If you are struggling with loneliness, it will help you to understand the true nature of loneliness. As we learned in a previous chapter about depression, don't confuse loneliness with other similar conditions. For instance, realize that loneliness is not the same thing as being alone. Actually, it is healthy for us to experience frequent seasons of solitude. Jesus was extremely busy, surrounded by mobs daily. In the midst of His busy schedule, He maintained the habit of getting alone for a quiet time to communicate with His Father. Simply because you enjoy solitude doesn't mean you are suffering from loneliness.

........................................................................

# Simply because you enjoy solitude doesn't mean you are suffering from loneliness.

........................................................................

I enjoy fishing. One of the main reasons I like it is to get alone in the beauty of God's creation. It is refreshing to be still and quiet and meditate on His Word. That's the reason a lot of people enjoy going to the mountains and sitting alone, viewing the gorgeous panorama of God's creation. For the same reason, others enjoy sitting alone on a beach gazing at a serene sunset. Solitude is not loneliness. We often discover tranquility in solitude.

Loneliness should not be confused with homesickness. A college student away from home may experience a deep longing to be reunited with his family. A soldier stationed overseas experiences homesickness. A traveling sales representative who spends much of his time away from his family will feel the magnetic pull to get back home. This is not critical loneliness, because these people have a home to which they may return. They are only temporarily alone.

However, loneliness is a feeling of being unneeded, unloved, unwanted, and even unnecessary. It is a desperate sense of being out of touch with those around us. Job experienced tragic sorrow that produced his intolerable loneliness. Although people surrounded him, he was still lonely. Have you ever experienced any of the following thoughts? "Nobody needs me." "Nobody wants me." "Nobody loves me." "I am just not important in the world."

### Isolation

Isn't it strange that in an age when there are more people on earth who are more connected through the Internet than ever before in our history, people are lonelier than ever? Cities are simply places where thousands of people can be lonely together. Every high-rise apartment is a monument to loneliness. Behind many of the doors of homes and apartments in your city are people who are aching from loneliness. Lonely people often gravitate to shopping malls just for the opportunity to be around other people. Our impersonal society only aggravates the problem where we are known more as a taxpayer identity number than a person with a name.

## Behind many of the doors of homes and apartments in your city are people who are aching from loneliness.

Loneliness is most often expressed by a sense of deep melancholy. However, loneliness is also sometimes reflected in a poor self-image that results in violent anger directed toward others. In extreme cases, it can often drive people to commit terrible atrocities. On Wednesday, October 16, 1991, George Hennard savagely vented his anger, frustration, and loneliness. He drove his truck through the window of a cafeteria and then calmly began to shoot the diners. Before he took his own life, he had killed 24 people and wounded 22 others. Criminal psychologists could spend many years trying to determine what twisted motive caused such a bizarre act. Evidence indicates that his desperate loneliness was a compelling factor in his actions. Since that time, random mass killings have become the norm. In recent years, there have been dozens of school and workplace shootings by young and old who often turn out to be loners with no real social connections.

## Rejection

Since earliest childhood, we have wanted to be liked and accepted by our peers. When playground friends chose sides for kickball, nobody wanted to be the last one picked! As we grew older, we tried to be accepted into a certain circle of friends, willing to do almost anything to gain that acceptance. As we become adults, we often never fully shake the desire to be accepted in our jobs and among new friends. We "friend" people on Facebook and hope that they'll accept us. Advertisers spend millions every year just trying to get someone to "like" a certain product. Rejection can damage us emotionally and produce loneliness.

> As we become adults, we often never fully shake the desire to be accepted in our jobs and among new friends.

Divorced people often fight enduring battles against chronic loneliness. As a pastor, I have known far too many couples considering divorce. Although divorce is seldom 100 percent the fault of one of the partners, there is often a spouse who wants a divorce while the other does not. One spouse may be the subject of the divorce, while the other is the object of the divorce. Divorce produces an intense feeling of rejection at one of the deepest levels of the human psyche.

## Insecurity

Insecurity may also produce loneliness. If you don't possess a healthy self-image, you may be convinced that you aren't worth loving. If you don't love yourself, you suspect that others can't love you either. Insecure people tend to build walls around themselves rather than build bridges toward other people. (See Chapter 7 on improving your self-image.)

......................................................................

# A person who loves himself understands that he is valuable because God loves him.

......................................................................

In Matthew 19:19, Jesus told us to love our neighbor as we love ourselves. There is a difference between loving oneself and being "in love" with oneself. A person who is in love with himself has a problem with selfish egotism. He stands in front of a mirror and sings, "How great thou art!" On the other hand, a person who loves himself understands that he is valuable because God loves him. You are always somebody special because God loves you so very much.

Lonely people react to their loneliness in a variety of ways. Some overeat because they need comfort. Others don't eat enough for the same reason. Some struggle with lingering insomnia due to loneliness, while others can't get out of bed. Some consume alcohol and abuse drugs because of their loneliness. The answer to loneliness is not in a bottle or pill, but in a Person. His name is Jesus Christ. Consider how Jesus can ease and erase your loneliness.

## CONQUERING YOUR LONELINESS

Most psychologists agree that we possess three basic human needs. First, we all have a need to love and to be loved. Second, we all have a need to be understood and accepted by someone else. Third, we all desire to be needed and wanted. A lonely person feels that these basic needs are being neglected.[9] Let's see how Jesus Christ can fulfill these three basic needs.

Your journey out of loneliness begins by realizing that Jesus loves you unconditionally. He loves you more than your parents love you. He loves you more than your spouse loves you. I am thrilled every time I think that Jesus knows me better than anyone, and yet He still loves me more than anyone else does. He loves you, warts and all. Our omniscient Lord not only knows all of our past mistakes, He knows all the mistakes we will make in the future. And yet, He still loves us. That is the kind of love you can't resist.

••••••••••••••••••••••••••••••••••••••••••••••••••••••••

## Your journey out of loneliness begins by realizing that Jesus loves you unconditionally.

••••••••••••••••••••••••••••••••••••••••••••••••••••••••

Consider how Jesus can meet your second basic need. He understands you and accepts you. He understands your loneliness because He too experienced bitter loneliness. The prophet Isaiah portrayed the utter rejection of Jesus the Messiah: "He grew up before him like a tender shoot, and like a root out of dry ground. He had no beauty or majesty to attract us to him, nothing in his appearance that we should desire him. He was despised and rejected by men, a man of sorrows and familiar with suffering. Like one from whom men hide their faces he was despised and we esteemed him not." (Isaiah 53:2-3) Jesus' closest friends left Him all alone on the night that He needed them most, so He can understand your loneliness.

As you read this, you may be relaxing in the comfort of your home. Remember that Jesus didn't enjoy having a place to call home. He said, "Foxes have holes and birds of the air have nests, but the Son of Man has no place to lay his head." (Luke 9:58) Jesus wants to relieve

---

9    Adrian Rogers, *Mastering Your Emotions* (Nashville, Tennessee: Broadman Press, 1988), p. 101.

your loneliness. He is willing to accept you into His family. Before you ever accepted Christ, Christ accepted you. You will never experience rejection from Him when you come to Him in humility and faith.

Our third basic human need is to be wanted. I recall that as I was growing up, I saw a large sign in the post office with a picture of Uncle Sam pointing his finger and saying, "Uncle Sam wants you." In reality, Jesus Christ is pointing His nail-pierced hand at you and saying, "I want you." He wants you to follow Him. He wants you to serve Him. Jesus wants you to carry out His work here on this earth. You are important to Him.

In Luke 19, we meet a wealthy but lonely man named Zacchaeus. If he were alive today, no one would accept a friend request from Zacchaeus on Facebook. When Jesus came to his city, Zacchaeus climbed up in a tree to have a better view, presumably happy to be away from the crowd below. Jesus looked up and said, "Zacchaeus, come down immediately. I must stay at your house today." (Luke 19:5) As Zacchaeus climbed down from that tree, he must have marveled that Jesus, of all people, wanted to be with him. How did He know him by name? Zacchaeus didn't know. In your darkest hours, Jesus comes to you and calls you by name. He says, "I love you, I understand your pain, and I want you to be My friend."

............................................................

## Jesus wants you to carry out His work here on this earth. You are important to Him.

............................................................

You may be thinking that this is all so spiritual that you cannot really understand it. You may be like the little boy who called out for his mother in the middle of the night during a storm. She came in and assured him that God was there with him in his room. The child looked up at his mother and said, "I know God is here, but I want somebody with skin on!" Likewise, you may be thinking, "I need somebody real. I need somebody who is here, right now!"

That may be part of your problem. Until you understand that Jesus Christ *is* real and that Jesus *is* here now, you will not conquer your feelings of loneliness. You must affirm that Jesus Christ is more real than these words you are reading. In fact, He is there with you right now. In your loneliness, don't visit some "lonely hearts" website looking for companionship. Look to Jesus Christ. He is the first step out of loneliness.

........................................................................

# You must affirm that Jesus Christ is more real than these words you are reading.

........................................................................

After Jesus liberates you from loneliness, you are free to seek human companionship. You shouldn't just wait for another person to enter your life; perhaps you should journey into another person's life. Why don't you seek out someone to help and establish a new friendship? It will help to prevent the recurrence of loneliness, and it will fill another person's lonely hours as well.

If you are lonely and would like to do something about it, consider these helpful suggestions:[10]

(1) Keep moving. Don't let a week go by without giving or accepting an invitation from another person. If no one calls you, call someone.

(2) Practice speaking to new people. If necessary, learn lines in advance: what to say at parties, suppers, etc.

(3) Remember, the easiest social skill, and the most enduring, is

---

10   Dr. Allan Fromme, Quoted from Lloyd Cory, *Quotable Quotations* (Wheaton, Illinois: Victor Books, 1985), p. 221.

to know how to listen.

(4) Remember that "making a habit of people" means finding every possible way to be with people, to do things with people, to become involved with people.

Try being part of a small group experience. You can generally find a small support group in your church. If you simply attend a large worship service and go home again, your loneliness will not be dispelled. Find a small group of people who will allow you to join them for Christian fellowship. Many churches provide Sunday school classes or support groups. Don't wait for others to come to you; initiate the contact yourself.

## A FINAL WORD TO THOSE WHO ARE NOT LONELY

If you are thinking, "My problem is certainly not loneliness; in fact, I have so many people pulling on me all the time that I can't find solitude." Perhaps you should consider looking around for someone who may be lonely. Would you be willing to include a person like that in your circle of friends? You are never more like the Lord Jesus than when you seek out a lonely person and provide genuine friendship.

........................................................................

You are never more like the Lord Jesus than when you seek out a lonely person and provide genuine friendship.

........................................................................

I once knew a dear widow who had lived alone for 20 years. I asked her, "How do you cope with loneliness?" She smiled and said, "Whenever I start feeling blue and lonely, I take out my egg timer and set it for five minutes. I sit down and feel sorry for myself until the bell rings. Then I get up, smile, get busy, and sing this old song:

> I've seen the lightning flashing, I've heard the thunder roll.
> I've felt sin's breakers dashing, trying to conquer my soul.
> I've heard the voice of Jesus telling me still to fight on.
> He promised never to leave me, never to leave me alone.
> No, never alone, no never alone.
> He promised never to leave me, never to leave me alone."[11]

---

11  Author unknown.

## TO THINK ABOUT:

- How can a person be in a relationship or in the middle of a crowd and still be lonely?

- How would you describe loneliness?

- What is the connection between a low self-esteem and loneliness?

- How does Jesus fulfill our basic human needs to be loved, understood, and needed?

- How would you encourage a lonely person to seek Jesus as his or her closest friend?

- Why is it not good for Christians to be isolated all the time?

- How can you reach out to a lonely person this week?


## FOR THE FOLLOWING SCRIPTURES, ASK:
○ What does it say?    ○ What does it mean?    ○ How can you apply it?

- Isaiah 41:10
- Matthew 11:28-30
- John 14:16-18

# CHAPTER 5

# Take Your Finger Off the Panic Button!

In over 40 years as a pastor, I have counseled with many people who complain of struggling with oppressive fear. A surprisingly large number of people have experienced panic attacks—sudden, overwhelming feelings of intense fear and stark panic. Their standard question to me is, "Am I going crazy?"

The National Institute of Health has concluded that panic disorder affects 6 million Americans.[12] According to their research, people with panic disorder may have:

- Sudden and repeated attacks of fear
- A feeling of being out of control during a panic attack
- An intense worry about when the next attack will happen
- A fear or avoidance of places where panic attacks have occurred in the past
- Physical symptoms during an attack, such as a pounding or racing heart, sweating, breathing problems, weakness or dizziness, feeling hot or a cold chill, tingly or numb hands, chest pain, or stomach pain.[13]

---

12  National Institute for Mental Health website, http://www.nimh.nih.gov/health/topics/panic-disorder/index.shtml, accessed August 19, 2013.
13  Ibid.

Haunting fear has been a reality since the introduction of sin in the world. Adam disobeyed God and for the first time felt the icy fingers of morbid fear clutching at his mind. He hid from God because he was afraid. (Genesis 3:10) Fear will always be a part of the sinful human experience.

······································································

# There are some healthy fears that should not be suppressed because they are there to protect us from harm.

······································································

Jesus predicted in Luke 21:26 that the time would come when people's hearts would fail them for fear. He described a time in the last days when people would literally be "scared to death."

All of us experience brief seasons of being afraid. We might have a close call at an intersection in the car, experience a health scare, or lie awake at night at the end of the month worrying if we'll have enough in the bank to cover the bills. All of those scary situations are just part of normal, everyday life. However, we need to recognize the chronic, crippling type of fear that keeps us in bondage.

## GOOD AND BAD FEAR

If you are struggling with fear, it will help you to understand there are two categories of fear: good bad and bad fear. You must learn how each one affects you and how you may overcome the bad, unhealthy kind of fear.

### Good Fear That Protects Us

In 1933, Franklin Delano Roosevelt served a fearful American public. Our nation was suffering a crippling economic depression with one out of every four men unemployed. Roosevelt himself knew how to face tough challenges since he had overcome the debilitating effects of polio as an adult. He spoke these memorable words to our nation as we faced an uncertain future: "The only thing we have to fear is fear itself." At the time, those words provided comfort to a struggling nation.

However, is that statement really true today? I think we *do* have things to fear "other than fear itself." There are some healthy fears that should not be suppressed because they are there to protect us from harm. For example, parents should teach their children to fear things that can harm them like rattlesnakes and poisonous spiders. Parents also teach their children to be wary of strangers. A healthy fear of danger can keep us safe.

### Fear of God

In Matthew 10:28, Jesus instructed us about another good kind of fear. He said, "Do not be afraid of those who kill the body but cannot kill the soul. Rather, be afraid of the One who can destroy both soul and body in hell." Jesus warns us that we will all face judgment. We should develop a healthy fear of the One who has the authority to execute judgment upon sin. If a person is not a Christian, he should face the hereafter with a sense of fear and trepidation. Death does not end the human existence. If you are a Christian and have accepted Christ into your heart, you need not fear judgment. God assures us in Romans 8:1 that there is no condemnation for those who are in Christ Jesus.

## If you are a Christian and have accepted Christ into your heart, you need not fear judgment.

An acrostic I use to describe the healthy kind of fear of God that the Bible teaches is F-E-A-R: the **F**ather **E**arns **A**we and **R**espect. Respecting our heavenly Father is certainly a good fear; being afraid of Him is not. The key to understanding healthy fear is found in Proverbs 9:10, "The fear of the Lord is the beginning of wisdom..." Reverent fear of God is a healthy, holy fear. We shouldn't cringe before the Lord and fear Him to the point that we never approach Him; rather, we must develop a holy reverence for the person and power of God.

········································································

## We must remember that He is the Almighty God, the Lord of the universe.

········································································

Fearing God is somewhat like fearing electricity. An experienced electrician must continually regard electricity with careful respect. Carelessness can lead to an accident or even death. While a skilled electrician must fear electricity, he is not afraid to work with it and use it. In our relationship with God, we should not exhibit casualness toward Him. We must maintain a sense of awe and respect for Him. People often refer to God as "the man upstairs" or "the good lord." We must remember that He is the Almighty God, the Lord of the universe. We should bow down before Him in honor and respect.

There is no contradiction between fearing God and loving God. The person who fears God the most loves Him the best. We are told by David, "The fear of the Lord is pure, enduring forever." (Psalm 19:9) This is the healthy kind of fear that we should develop toward God.

### Harmful Fear

Although some fear is healthy, there is a type of fear that is harmful. In 2 Timothy 1:7, Paul writes these words of encouragement to a terrified young preacher: "For God has not given us the spirit of fear; but of power, of love, and of a sound mind." (NKJV) Paul is referring to a condition that can destroy and enslave us. Psychologists have cataloged over 700 different fears. We call these fears "phobias," from the Greek word for fear. Phobias range from A to Z: from acrophobia (fear of heights) to zoophobia (fear of animals). People suffering from various emotional problems often find themselves in bondage to harmful fears as well.

The apostle Paul informs us that God did not give us this fear. If you are suffering from a compulsive fear, God did not give it to you. Chances are, it came from Satan, who is the sinister minister of fear. If you are struggling with an unidentified but unnerving fear, it may be helpful for you to learn about some of the most common phobias.

John Bisagno, former pastor of First Baptist Church, Houston, Texas, loves to tell the story about how he used to be afraid of flying. One day he went to a bus station to purchase a ticket to travel for a speaking engagement. The ticket agent recognized him. She asked him why he was riding the bus instead of flying.

After he responded that he was afraid to fly, she chided him for being so fearful. She asked, "Doesn't God say that He will be with you always?"

> There is no contradiction between fearing God and loving God. The person who fears God the most loves Him the best.

Bisagno responded, "That's not what the Bible says at all. God says, "Lo (low), I am with you always."

Most people are mildly fearful every time they get on an airplane. That is not a fear of heights. Acrophobia is a crippling fear that prevents a person from ever flying or even climbing to a high point. A friend who refused to fly once told me, "I'm not afraid of flying.

I'm afraid of falling." Is this kind of fear reasonable? You can be sure
that God did not give you this fear.

·········································································

# If you are suffering from a compulsive fear, God did not give it to you. Chances are, it came from Satan, who is the sinister minister of fear.

·········································································

Other people suffer from claustrophobia. This is a compulsive
fear of enclosed spaces. A person suffering from claustrophobia
cannot stand to be confined in tight quarters. He is afraid of closets,
elevators, or small rooms. Sometimes a person with claustrophobia
will not fly because of the fear of being shut up in an airplane.
I once knew a sweet Christian lady who suffered terribly from
claustrophobia. Once while we were traveling on a bus on a mission
project she rushed up to my seat with a frantic look in her eyes. She
was flushed and trembling. She said, "Have you seen the road signs?
We are approaching a tunnel, and I can't stand it."

As the tunnel loomed ahead of us, she quickly shared that she was
claustrophobic. Just the thought of being in a tunnel frightened her
beyond reason. She begged me to stop the bus so she could get off.
She was more willing to look for another route to bypass the tunnel
than to travel through it on our bus.

I finally convinced her to remain on the bus. Another lady held
her hand and prayed for her during the two minutes it took to travel
through the tunnel. By shutting her eyes tightly and praying, she was
able to conquer her fear. After a while, I was able to talk her through
her fears. She admitted this was an unreasonable "spirit of fear" that
did not come from God. On the return trip, she was able to face her
fear with faith. In the tunnel, she smiled with her eyes wide open and
felt that she had accomplished a great feat by eliminating her fear.

Agoraphobia is almost the opposite of claustrophobia. It is the fear of being in a crowd. If you are suffering from this phobia, you have a continual desire to stay in your home, in your own cocoon of safety. Agoraphobia makes it difficult to leave home, travel, or be at an event like a concert or fair. This is often accompanied by harrowing panic attacks. Many people also suffer from pathophobia, which is a fear of germs and contagious illnesses. A person with pathophobia doesn't want to shake your hand, but if he does, he will hurry to wash his hands as soon as possible. Pathophobia often leads to hypochondria—a fixation with being sick. Most people have learned not to ask a hypochondriac, "How are you feeling?"

According to many studies, the most common fear among Americans is kerugmaphobia (from the Greek word for *preaching*). This is the fear of public speaking. People often complain that they break out in a cold sweat and their pulse increases any time they speak to an audience. Have you discovered that the human brain is an amazing organ? It starts working the minute you are born and doesn't stop until you stand up in front of a crowd to speak!

···········································································

# If you are suffering from these or other phobias, you should identify them and admit your fears.

···········································································

These are just a few of the dozens of harmful fears psychiatrists have identified. If you are suffering from these or other phobias, you should identify them and admit your fears. Seek professional help from a trained counselor, if necessary. Only then will you be able to subdue these irrational feelings.

## THE HARMFUL EFFECTS OF FEAR

If you don't face your fears and deal honestly with them, you will
continue to suffer the clutching turmoil that fear produces. In the
Bible, young Timothy is a good example of the damaging impact
of fear. Timothy was pastoring the church in Ephesus when Paul
wrote his letters to him. Paul wrote to encourage Timothy because
he had experienced fear and failure. Fear had minimized Timothy's
effectiveness, just as it will minimize your ability to accomplish all
that God wants you to do.

### Fear Causes You to Discount God's Care

One harmful effect of fear is that it will cause you to overlook
God's care and protection. Timothy had forgotten his wonderful
heritage and his blessing from God, so Paul encouraged Timothy to
remember he had powerful gifts for ministry and acknowledged that
he came from a strong line of courageous believers (2 Timothy 1:5).
We, too, are prone to forget God's abundant goodness when we are
suffering from fear.

> One harmful effect of fear is that
> it will cause you to overlook God's
> care and protection.

In 1974, I was in Israel participating in an archeological study
with other students from Samford University in Birmingham,
Alabama. We were there during the Yom Kippur War. There was a
tremendous amount of tension. Each day we could hear fighter jets
roaring overhead and artillery pounding in the distance. During
our last week in Jerusalem, a radical terrorist from the P.L.O. stole
a portable Surface-To-Air missile and publicly threatened to shoot
down an El Al Airline flight. We were scheduled to fly out of
Jerusalem on the following Friday morning on El Al Airline. As the

day of departure approached, we grew more fearful by the hour. I gathered with about 12 of my classmates on the night before we were scheduled to leave. We wanted to have a prayer meeting, but it turned into a "scare meeting" instead. Everyone talked about his or her fears—expecting the worst. One of my married friends wept openly, saying that he doubted he would never see his wife and child again. A contagious spirit of insidious fear spread like a cold fog in our midst.

> I had simply forgotten God's word of encouragement. Fear will make you forget God's promises.

I went to bed that night literally shaking! Of course, I couldn't sleep. My stomach was churning and my brain was racing as I tossed and turned. About midnight, I got up and stared out the window. As I gazed into heaven, it seemed as if God asked me a question. He seemed to say, "David, have you forgotten my word in Psalm 27:1?" It was a verse I had recently memorized.

I began to quote, "The Lord is my light and my salvation—whom shall I fear? The Lord is the stronghold of my life—of whom shall I be afraid?" In His Word, God was telling me that He would take care of me. Suddenly my irrational fear and excessive anxiety vanished. I returned to bed and slept soundly, trusting that God's promise was reliable. We departed safely from Jerusalem and returned to America. I had simply forgotten God's word of encouragement. Fear will make you forget God's promises.

### Fear Hampers Success

Fear will also hinder your success in life. It will cause you to fail when otherwise you would be successful. I believe young Timothy was fearful because he knew that Paul was imprisoned for preaching the Gospel. Since Paul was his model for ministry, Timothy was afraid that he would soon be arrested and imprisoned, too! This nagging, crippling fear prevented him from being and doing his best for God.

........................................................................

# I have known many Christians who have allowed fear to prevent their obedient service for God.

........................................................................

Fear can have the same negative impact upon us. An athlete who is afraid usually will perform poorly. A basketball player who is afraid to shoot will often miss crucial shots. I recall a high school friend who failed her driving test three times because of her distress. She was an intelligent person who could drive well, but terror caused her to "freeze up" when she took the test. Fear and failure are first cousins. They always run together.

In Matthew 25, Jesus related the story of a master who gave various talents to his three servants and then left town. When the master returned, he demanded an accounting. The servants who had received five and two talents had taken that money, invested it, and had gained a 100 percent return for the master. Their master was pleased and complimented them for their courageous stewardship. When the master confronted the servant who had received one talent, there was no increase. The servant made this excuse, "I was afraid and I went out and hid your talent in the ground." The master was infuriated and replied, "You wicked, lazy servant." Fear had caused him to fail.

I have known many Christians who have allowed fear to prevent their obedient service for God. Like the three servants, we will have to give an accounting of what we did with all the blessings and opportunities He gives us. Don't let your doubts force you to bury your God-given abilities. We must never be afraid to attempt great things for God. Some people go through life so afraid of making a mistake that their entire lives are a mistake. They have missed out on so much! Don't let fear keep you from attempting what may seem to be impossible. Walt Disney was fired from his first job as a newspaper cartoonist. A newspaper editor told him that he had no future in cartoons! Disney declared bankruptcy four times before he finally succeeded. He did not let fear and failure stand in the way of his dreams and goals.

### Fear Can Harm Your Health

Fear will also affect you physically. There is a direct correlation between anxiety, fear, and physical illness. According to 1 Timothy 5:23, young Timothy was often sick. I believe that Timothy was weaker than he should have been because of his anxiety.

A prominent physician spoke these words at a symposium on psychosomatic illness (a physical illness that is tied to emotional distress). "In spite of what they say, 90 percent of the chronic patients who see today's physicians have one common problem. Their problem did not start with a cough, or chest pain, or hyperacidity…the first symptom was fear."[14]

······································································

## Don't let fear keep you from attempting what may seem to be impossible.

······································································

You may get ulcers from what you eat, but sometimes they result from what is eating you. "A cheerful heart is good medicine, but a crushed spirit dries up the bones." (Proverbs 17:22) According to the Bible, there is a strong connection between your attitude and your physical health. A cheerful heart affects us like good medicine, but

14  Adrian Rogers, *Mastering Your Emotions* (Nashville, Tennessee: Broadman Press, 1988), p. 117.

an anxious, fearful spirit produces pain and weakness. Healthcare professionals agree that fear and worry affect us in many negative ways. How long will you allow your life to be influenced by a spirit of fear that is unreasonable and illogical? Although irrational fear does not come from God, there is hope and there is help in His Word.

## CONQUERING YOUR FEARS

In order to understand the secret to conquering your fears, let's go back to 2 Timothy 1:7 and see that God has given us three tools to replace our fear. He gives us a spirit of "power, of love, and of a sound mind." (NKJV) These are the weapons supplied to us by our Father to face and fight fear with faith.

. . . . . . . . . . . . . . . . . . . . . . . . . . . . . . . . . . . . . . . . . . . . . . . . . . . . .

Although irrational fear does not come from God, there is hope and there is help in His Word.

. . . . . . . . . . . . . . . . . . . . . . . . . . . . . . . . . . . . . . . . . . . . . . . . . . . . .

*Power*

If you are struggling with an inordinate fear that causes you to adjust your lifestyle, God has promised to supply you with His power to overcome. Without the promise of His power, we would be victimized by constant dread. In the dramatic story of David and Goliath, a godless, nine-foot-tall giant stood and challenged the Israelites to a fight, and the Bible says that they all ran from him in terror. (1 Samuel 17:25) A contagious fear infiltrated the entire camp like a plague. But little David understood the promise of God's supernatural power. Armed with only a slingshot and some stones, he confronted the ugly giant in battle. David declared, "I come against you in the name of the Lord Almighty, the God of the armies of Israel, whom you have defied. This day the Lord will hand you over to me." (1 Samuel 17:45-46) Certainly David must have been afraid, but God's power helped him overcome his feelings.

We often face "Goliaths" who stand up and prohibit us from proceeding in life. It is at these times when we must depend upon God's supernatural power. His power is available to banish whatever is holding you back—it is "made perfect in our weakness." (2 Corinthians 12:9)

*Love*

God also promises to provide us His love to overcome our fears. "Perfect love drives out fear." (1 John 4:18) God's perfect love for us removes the uncertainty of fear. Also, our love for God, though it is not perfect, helps us to overcome our fears.

I've read many stories about mothers who experience supernatural courage and strength in defending their child in scary situations like a dog attack or a burning car. If her child is threatened, the typical mother will overcome her own fears to protect her child. Her love for her child overrides her fear of the situation. Even so, our love for God helps us to overcome our fears. Knowing that God loves us and that all things work together for good to them that love Him, we find strength to face fear with faith.

···································································

## Without the promise of His power, we would be victimized by constant dread.

···································································

The apostle John had personally experienced the perfect love of Jesus. Later in his life when he was imprisoned on Patmos, he had an experience with the living Lord that changed him forever. In his vision of the resurrected, glorified Christ, John fell down at His feet as a dead man. Fear (the Father Earns Awe and Respect) caused him to fall prostrate before the Lord. According to Revelation 1:17, Jesus laid His right hand on John and tenderly said, "Do not be afraid. I am the First and the Last." John experienced the power of unconditional love to overcome fear. Likewise, whenever we fall victim to fear, Jesus places His loving hand on us to reassure us. John was no longer afraid because he knew Jesus loved him so completely. The same emotions that channel fear can also channel love.[15] God's kind of love is pure, unchanging, and permanent. It is the "perfect" tool for calming our fears.

### Sound Mind

The third supernatural resource to battle fear is a sound mind. This phrase literally means to "exercise self-discipline." It is the God-given ability to distinguish between healthy and harmful fears. It enables us to know which fears can be overcome by God's power and which are really empty threats. Zig Ziglar is credited with this definition of fear: "F.E.A.R. is False Evidence Appearing Real."

····························································

## God has given us a sound mind to be able to distinguish between healthy fear and those fears that paralyze us.

····························································

Early one morning I was getting dressed to leave for work before sunrise. I had kept all the lights in our bedroom off in order not to awaken my wife. The house was dark and quiet. After I had dressed, I was getting ready to leave our bedroom and I suddenly saw a man standing outside our bedroom door. Immediately, the icy fingers of fear gripped my throat. In the dim light, I could barely detect that the intruder was ugly, standing there crouched and threatening. I didn't know whether to shout or run. I slowly lifted my hand to

---

15  Lloyd John Ogilvie, *The Bush Is Still Burning* (Waco, Texas: Word Books, 1980), p. 45.

defend myself and as I did, he lifted his hand to attack. In a sudden flash of foolish realization, I understood I was looking at the back of the bedroom door where we'd hung a full-length mirror! The nasty intruder was really my own reflection! The fear was real, but the cause of fear was only a reflection of something sinister.

As you examine your own fears, ask yourself whether or not those fears are legitimate. God has given us a sound mind to be able to distinguish between healthy fear and those fears that paralyze us. With power, love, and a sound mind, you can conquer your fears.

## TO THINK ABOUT:

- How would you explain the "fear of God" to someone?

- On a scale of 1-5, how much does fear influence your decisions? (1 – very much, 5 – not much) Explain.

- How can irrational fear make you doubt how much God cares for you?

- What is your typical response to fear?

- When was a time you relied on God's power to deal with a specific fear?

- How does God's love override fear?

- Why does it take practice and self-discipline to erase most of our fears?

## FOR THE FOLLOWING SCRIPTURES, ASK:

○ What does it say?    ○ What does it mean?    ○ How can you apply it?

- Proverbs 1:7
- 2 Timothy 1:7
- 1 John 4:18

# CHAPTER 6

# God's Antidotes for the Poison of Anxiety

A man once remarked to me, "Don't tell me that worry doesn't work. It must work, because most of the things I worry about never happen!" Truthfully, we waste a lot of precious time worrying about things that never occur. Henry Ward Beecher once wrote, "It is not work that kills men. It is worry. Work is healthy; worry is like rust upon the blade."[16]

In an encouraging passage of Scripture written to the Christians at Philippi, Paul gives us clear directions to dispel worry. He writes:

> Rejoice in the Lord always. I will say it again: Rejoice! Let your gentleness be evident to all. The Lord is near. Do not be anxious about anything, but in everything, by prayer and petition, with thanksgiving, present your requests to God. And the peace of God, which transcends all understanding, will guard your hearts and minds in Christ Jesus. Finally, brothers, whatever is true, whatever is noble, whatever is right, whatever is pure, whatever is lovely, whatever is admirable—if anything is excellent or praiseworthy—think about such things. (Philippians 4:4-8)

Anxiety is a poison, but there are five antidotes in this passage of Scripture to help us overcome its toxic effects.

---

16  Eleanor Kirk, *Beecher As A Humorist* (New York: Fords, Howard, and Halbert, 1987), p. 81.

## REJOICE IN THE LORD

First, we are instructed to rejoice in the Lord. You may be cynical about rejoicing because your problems seem such that you cannot rejoice. You may be thinking that it's easy for others to rejoice, but you have no reason to do so. Like many people, you may object, "If you knew *my* problems, you wouldn't tell *me* to rejoice!"

············································································

## You may be cynical about rejoicing because your problems seem such that you cannot rejoice.

············································································

Let me remind you that the one instructing us to rejoice is the apostle Paul. When Paul wrote these words, he was not a professor in a theological seminary, safe within his educational cloister. He didn't write his instructions while seated in tranquility atop a mountain peak, gazing over the snow-capped Alps. He didn't write this letter while lounging on a tropical beach, allowing the waves and soft wind to massage his tired body. When he wrote the words, "Rejoice in the Lord," he was a prisoner in a dark, damp dungeon of the Roman Empire. There was a death sentence on his head. Every time he heard the heavy footfall of the soldiers walking down the stone corridors outside his cell, he must have wondered if at that moment they were coming to drag him away for execution. Here in prison, shut off from his loved ones and facing death, Paul wrote the most counterintuitive advice imaginable: "Rejoice in the Lord always!"

### Rejoicing Is a Choice

Whatever your problems are, or whatever you may be facing, is it any worse than what Paul was facing? Sure, it's easy to rejoice when all your circumstances are ideal. Anyone can do that. It takes real faith to rejoice when you meet utter devastation head on. In those times, you may be tempted to say, "I don't want to rejoice because

I don't *feel* like rejoicing." Feeling has absolutely nothing to do with rejoicing. A mature believer has made the discovery that one must make the choice to rejoice. We choose to rejoice regardless of how we feel or how people may treat us.

The Psalmist says, "This is the day the Lord has made, let us rejoice and be glad in it." (Psalm 118:24) The Psalmist didn't say, "I will rejoice and be glad if I feel like it or if everything is going well." Neither did he write, "I will rejoice if all my friends treat me well and if I have a fat bank account." His only basis for joy was that God had made the day. You, too, can make a similar decision. When you are facing a difficult problem, you can choose to be sad, frown, and complain about it. You can choose to worry about it until you are sick, or you can make your choice to rejoice in the Lord. It is simply up to you.

> ## We choose to rejoice regardless of how we feel or how people may treat us.

When people are asked, "How are you doing?" they often respond, "I'm doing all right under the circumstances." What are they doing there under the circumstances? We are informed in Ephesians 2:6 that we are "seated with Him in the heavenly realms." We should not be *under* the circumstances; we should be on top of them! Circumstances are like a mattress. If you get under them, you may be smothered, but when you get on top of them you have the ability to rest and rejoice. Take a moment and claim that you are safely in Christ, far above your circumstances.

### God Is Good, Despite the Pain

Will you apply this command to a problem that you are worrying about at this moment? Have you been able to rejoice in the midst of your difficulty? If you haven't, try saying, "Praise the Lord" ten times aloud as you meditate and pray about your problem. It will be difficult to do this without finding a smile creep across your face. This command to greatly rejoice doesn't ignore pain or deny that bad things happen. Nor is it rejoicing over the bad things that happen. This doesn't mean you say, "I'm so happy that I lost my job!" No, you aren't rejoicing over your misfortune; you are recognizing that in the midst of pain and suffering, God is good, and His love for you is unfailing.

## REFUSE TO BE ANXIOUS

The second antidote against the poison of anxiety is to refuse to be anxious about anything. The word "anxious" is the Greek word *merimnao*. It literally means to have your mind divided. As a believer, you will approach your problems with either faith or worry. When your mind is divided about how you should react, it produces undue anxiety. When you have a divided mind, you are rejoicing in the Lord one moment and then worrying about your problem in the very next moment. No wonder you're upset!

........................................................................

This command to greatly rejoice doesn't ignore pain or deny that bad things happen.

........................................................................

Jesus said, "Therefore do not worry about tomorrow, for tomorrow will worry about itself. Each day has enough trouble of its own." (Matthew 6:34) Worry accomplishes nothing and is a total waste of our time and energy. There are two days about which you should never worry: yesterday and tomorrow. There are two categories of things about which you should never worry: those things that you can do something about and those things about which you can do nothing. If there is something you can do about a problem, do it. If there is nothing you can do, don't worry about it.

........................................................................

# If there is something you can do about a problem, do it. If there is nothing you can do, don't worry about it.

........................................................................

The unknown author of this little poem understood this principle:

> For every evil under the sun,
> Either there is a cure,
> Or there is none.
> If there be one,
> Seek until you find it.
> If there be none,
> Never mind it.

### Worry Is Harmful

Chronic worry is like garbage that can clutter up your life. We all deal with mental, emotional, and spiritual garbage. A healthy believer continually disposes of this garbage, but an abnormally anxious person allows this garbage to accumulate. *Hoarders* is a popular show on television about the secret lives of real people who obsessively accumulate junk inside their home. Some families have garbage and debris piled so high inside their homes that they must carve pathways to get from room to room. They don't haul in other people's garbage; it is all theirs.

That's a graphic picture of worry. It's emotional garbage that you allow to accumulate in your mind. If you don't deal with it and dispose of it, it causes problems. Deep-seated worry can even be harmful to your emotional and physical health. Dr. Charles Mayo, the founder of the Mayo Clinic, wrote: "Worry affects the circulation, the heart, the digestive system, and the entire nervous system. I've never known a person to die of overwork, but many who died from worry." Our English word *worry* is derived from an older German word *wurgen*, meaning "to choke." The term has come to be used to denote "mental strangulation" to describe the harmful effects of worry.[17] Do you ever feel as if anxiety is strangling your mind?

### Worry Is a Sin

Is worry that serious? The Bible says, "Everything that does not come from faith is sin." (Romans 14:23) The opposite of worry is faith. Whenever we approach a situation, we can grab it by the handle of faith or the handle of worry. Faith is the end of anxiety, and anxiety is the end of faith. Faith and worry are mutually exclusive. You can experience one or the other but not both at the same time.

> Whenever we approach a situation, we can grab it by the handle of faith or the handle of worry.

Worry is a sin because it basically infers that God is a liar. God has promised to love us and to take care of us. (Psalm 121:7) He has promised that all things will work together for our good. (Romans 8:28) He has invited us to cast our burdens upon Him because He cares for us. (1 Peter 5:7) Whenever we worry, we are suggesting that God can neither be trusted, nor can He fulfill His promises.

---

17  Quoted from Lloyd Cory, *Quotable Quotations* (Wheaton, Illinois: Victor Books, 1985), p. 445.

Many evangelical Christians would never commit adultery, steal, or commit gross sins of the flesh, and yet they are chronic worriers. You will not have victory over your worry until you admit that it is as sinful as any other sin in God's eyes.

........................................................................

# Whenever we worry, we are suggesting that God can neither be trusted, nor can He fulfill His promises.

........................................................................

When I travel to Uganda, I am amazed by the variety of colorful birds that are all around. Many times, I see species I have never seen before. In Matthew 6, Jesus challenged us to observe the birds of the sky and notice that birds never worry. An unknown author has written a poem describing an imaginary conversation between two birds:

> Said the robin to the sparrow,
> "I'd really like to know,
> Why these silly human creatures
> Rush about and worry so."
> Said the sparrow to the robin,
> "I think that it must be,
> That they have no heavenly father,
> Such as cares for you and me."

Just as God has promised to take care of the birds of the air, He has promised to take care of us because we are evermore precious to Him.

Wouldn't it be wonderful if you could hire someone who would do all of your worrying for you? There is a funny story about a man who was constantly worrying. He had a hard time relaxing and even suffered from ulcers. He worried about everything and anything. One day when he arrived at work, his countenance was totally changed. There was a bounce to his step and a smile on his face. A co-worker commented to him on the change, "What's happened to you? You used to worry all the time and now you seem so happy. What happened?"

The man said, "I've made a wonderful discovery. I have hired a professional worrier. I hired him to worry for me, and I pay him to worry about all my problems."

The friend responded, "That's a great idea. How much do you have to pay him?"

"Well, I pay him a thousand dollars a week."

His friend looked perplexed and said, "You don't make anywhere near that kind of money. How in the world are you going to pay him?"

The ex-worrywart simply smiled and said, "That's his worry, not mine!"

---

## You can lay your burden at the feet of the Lord, and it won't cost you a penny.

---

Wouldn't it be terrific if you could take any problem, give it to someone else and say, "I'm not going to worry any longer. I'll let you worry about it."? The glorious truth is that you can do that. You can lay your burden at the feet of the Lord, and it won't cost you a penny. Jesus has invited us to come to Him so that we can find "rest" for our souls. (Matthew 11:28-29)

## REPLACE WORRY WITH PRAYER

Many of you are going to have a lot of time on your hands if you seriously commit to not worrying. What will you do with all the minutes you used to spend every day worrying? The first antidote

against the poison of anxiety is to choose. Choose to rejoice. The
second is to refuse. Refuse to worry. If you try those two things and
you are still sick with worry, Paul suggests a third remedy: exchange
worry for prayer. Philippians 4:6 says, "In everything by prayer and
petition, with thanksgiving, present your requests to God."

### Pray Generally

Paul mentions several kinds of prayer in this passage. First, he makes
reference to the kind of prayers that we often pray for general occasions.
It's a cover-all kind of prayer in which we ask God to bless general things
like our food, the Sunday offering, our missionaries, or other basic
concerns. It means that whenever your mind returns to neutral, it returns
to an attitude of prayerfulness. You're always praying throughout the day.

> Have you discovered that when you
> are praying about a problem, you
> cannot worry about it?

### Ask God for What You Need

The second kind of prayer he mentions is that of petition or
supplication. That's a reference to personal, private prayer when
you spend time alone with God, seeking His face and studying
His Word. Have you discovered that when you are praying about a
problem, you cannot worry about it? On the other hand, when you
are consumed with worry about a problem, you will find it difficult
to pray about it. The key to overcoming worry is to get alone with
God and pray about your problems. Tell Him what you need. That
kind of prayer can really make a difference.

### Be Thankful

The third kind of prayer Paul describes is thanksgiving. We are told
to pray, thanking God for the answers even before we receive them. The

New Living Bible paraphrases it this way: "Don't worry about anything; instead, pray about everything. Tell God what you need and thank Him for all He has done." (Philippians 4:6) Have you ever longed for a close, intimate friend who would care for you and listen to you with compassion as you shared your deepest fears? Jesus Christ offers to be that kind of friend to you. How often have you sung the words of this familiar hymn, without contemplating the powerful message?

> What a friend we have in Jesus,
> All our sins and griefs to bear.
> What a privilege to carry,
> Everything to God in prayer.
> Oh, what peace we often forfeit,
> Oh, what needless pain we bear.
> All because we do not carry
> Everything to God in prayer.[18]

We are told in 1 Thessalonians 5:18: "Give thanks in all circumstances, for this is God's will in Jesus Christ." Likewise, in Ephesians 5:20, we are instructed to always be giving thanks. It's so easy to thank God for His blessings. It's much harder to thank Him for His presence and love when we are going through tough times and trials.

• • • • • • • • • • • • • • • • • • • • • • • • • • • • • • • • • • • • • • • • • • • • • • •

## The key to overcoming worry is to get alone with God and pray about your problems

• • • • • • • • • • • • • • • • • • • • • • • • • • • • • • • • • • • • • • • • • • • • • • •

Ironically, sometimes we can successfully face the big crises of life, but then our insignificant problems trip us up! Years ago, I got up

---

18   "What A Friend We Have In Jesus" (Words: Scriven, Joseph, 1855).

early before sunrise to attend a weekly prayer service. As I was shaving,
I meditated on the verse for the day printed on my Scripture calendar,
Philippians 4:6. I was quoting the verse aloud and rejoicing in the
Lord, giving thanks for all things—expecting a wonderful day. To get
to my car, I had to walk through our darkened basement toward the
garage, not wanting to turn on the lights and awaken my family. I did
that often, and I knew the way almost by touch. The night before, my
two young daughters had been playing with a jogging trampoline—a
small, round trampoline that sits about eight inches off the floor. They
usually kept it in a far corner of the basement, but for some reason the
night before they had unintentionally left it right in my path. As I was
walking alone in that darkened basement praising God, I hit it and
stumbled. It seemed that I turned three somersaults before I finally
hit the floor! As you imagine any pastor would do, instead of yelling,
I simply picked up the trampoline…and gently tossed it about 30
feet across the room! Then I got in my car to drive to church for my
morning prayer meeting, but I was steaming mad.

## It's much harder to thank Him for His presence and love when we are going through tough times and trials.

I was halfway to the church when the Lord spoke to me in a still
small voice seemingly edged with humor, "Is that all it takes for you
to lose your joy? Are you still willing to thank Me and rejoice?"

It only took a second for me to realize that the Lord was teaching me
a lesson, so I began to look for ways to give thanks. I didn't thank Him
that I had tripped and fallen. Instead, I began to thank Him that I had
two beautiful girls who were healthy enough to play on a trampoline.
I thanked Him that I was not hurt. I even thanked Him that I had a
home in which I could fall. As I continued to thank God, it became
easier and easier to do so. Little by little, my smile returned and the joy

of the Lord reentered my life. That's just a small example, but when you can thank God in the midst of a problem, you have taken a giant step to overcome your worry. What is it that has been tripping you up lately?

## REJECT NEGATIVE THOUGHTS

If you really want to overcome anxiety, you'll be busy rejoicing in the Lord, refusing to let emotional garbage pile up in your mind, and replacing worry with prayer. Now Paul gives us a fourth, heavy-duty antidote when we are infected by worry. We must learn to reject negative thinking. In Philippians 4:8, Paul lists some positive things upon which we should focus our thoughts instead: whatever is true, noble, right, pure, lovely, admirable, excellent, or praiseworthy.

· · · · · · · · · · · · · · · · · · · · · · · · · · · · · · · · · · · · · · · · · · · · · · · · · ·

## If you always concentrate on negatives, you will be as frustrated as a chameleon in a box of Crayons.

· · · · · · · · · · · · · · · · · · · · · · · · · · · · · · · · · · · · · · · · · · · · · · · · · ·

What the world calls positive thinking is what Christians call faith-thinking. If you fill your mind with negative, stinking thinking, you will continually be a victim of gnawing worry. If you always concentrate on negatives, you will be as frustrated as a chameleon in a box of Crayons. Your emotions will go up and down constantly. However, if you will reject negative thinking and focus upon positive thoughts, you can experience victory.

### We Become Like What We Think About Most

Proverbs 23:7 says, "As he thinks in his heart, so is he…" (KJV). In other words, our thoughts are important to our emotional health because we really do become what we think about the most. I recall hearing about a fourteen-year-old boy sitting in a Sunday school class as his teacher expressed this principle. The teacher said, "Boys, whatever you think about the most, you will become." One of the teenage boys responded with a look of horror, saying, "You mean I'll become a girl?"

Worry operates within the arena of your mind. Your mind is the battleground in the war between faith and worry. Worry is like a drip that slowly begins, one drop at a time. If it isn't shut off, it gradually becomes a constant trickle, then a steady flow that can't be stopped. The drip of worry causes a crack in your mind, then a well-worn crevice, then a gully. It soon develops into a valley or even a grand canyon of fear. Thoughts of fear soon rush through your mind like white water rapids. This torrent of worry will carry away logical thoughts of peace. And it all starts with what you are thinking right now.

Have you noticed that when you are busy in some activity, worry seems to be crowded out? But when you are sitting alone or lying in bed at night, worry creeps in and begins its devious task. We can take control of our mind and surrender it to the Lordship of Christ. "We take captive every thought to make it obedient to Christ." (2 Corinthians 10:5) How well you control your thoughts will determine the proportion of worry in your mind. If you are experiencing trouble, you cannot overcome it by *not* thinking about that problem. Why not? The thing you're trying not to think about will inevitably fill your mind. For instance, if you have a problem with lust, and you are constantly saying to yourself, "Don't think about lust … don't think about lust," what will you think about? You will usually think lustful thoughts.

## Our thoughts are important to our emotional health because we really do become what we think about the most.

Let me demonstrate this by asking you to participate in a brief experiment. In the next few moments, I want you to try not to think about something. At this moment, don't think about ice cream.

That's right. Don't think about vanilla ice cream, and certainly don't think about it with chocolate syrup and a cherry on top! You're not thinking about ice cream, are you? Chances are, unless you are pretty strong willed, you had trouble *not* visualizing ice cream! Don't overcome a negative thought pattern by trying *not* to think about it.

···············································································

# How well you control your thoughts will determine the proportion of worry in your mind.

···············································································

### There Is Plenty of Positive to Focus On

Instead, overcome negative thoughts by replacing them with positive thoughts. Our brain can only latch onto one image at a time. Let's continue the experiment. In your mind's eye, visualize Jesus Christ hanging on the cross. See Him there with nails in His hands and feet, a crown of thorns upon His head, and a spear in His side. See Him as people are ridiculing and scorning Him. Notice the love and compassion in His eyes. As you pictured this beautiful scene, chances are you were unable to think about much else except Jesus. Focusing on Jesus is the key to overcoming worry. Philippians 4:8 is actually a one-verse biography of Jesus Christ. Jesus is "true, noble, right, pure, lovely, admirable, excellent and praiseworthy." Think about Him. As we run the race of life, we are to "fix our eyes on Jesus." (Hebrews 12:2)

Many people are in bondage to manifold worries that should have no power over them. Have you ever seen an elephant outside a circus tent? A small chain around his leg, attached to a wooden stake, can often restrain the huge animal. The elephant could simply lift his foot and easily pull the stake out of the ground. The stake doesn't hold him in place; his mind does. Why? As a young calf, the elephant was heavily chained to a stake driven deep into the ground. He tried to pull free, but couldn't, and he remembers the pain of those attempts. Over a period of time, he became conditioned to the belief that he can't escape. As a result, a small wooden stake is all it takes to keep him in place. Has that happened to you? Worry is in your mind, and you may be chained to it, thinking you cannot escape. You can pull up any stake that is limiting your life and get rid of crippling anxiety for good.

## RECEIVE GOD'S PEACE

We can choose to rejoice. We can refuse to worry. We can replace worry with prayer. We can even learn to reject our negative thoughts. However, the final antidote to deal with the deadly virus of anxiety is not something we do it all—it is all God's doing. Philippians 4:7 tells us, "And the peace of God, which transcends all understanding, shall guard your hearts and your minds." Since worry operates in the mind, we need someone to guard our minds, and God has offered to do that. Not only was Paul in prison when he wrote these words— he was chained to a Roman soldier 24-7! As he glanced over at his constant companion, he must have thought, "It is possible for God's peace to guard me just as this Roman soldier is guarding me now."

> Worry is in your mind, and you may be chained to it, thinking you cannot escape.

Whenever the President of the United States makes an appearance, there are numerous secret service agents standing guard in the crowd with sunglasses on, talking into nearly invisible radio units. Everyone knows that they have automatic weapons underneath their coats. They are on guard against anything that will threaten the President. In the same way, if we allow it, God's peace will vigilantly surround us and protect our minds. Have you received His offer of peace?

Some people think that peace is the absence of problems. That's not true. You may think that you will have peace when your blood pressure goes down, when you get a good job, when all of your bills are paid, when you have no more problems with your children, and everyone loves you. That's not peace; that's heaven! Peace is not the absence of problems; peace is strength to deal with your problems. Jesus said, "I have told you these things, so that in me you may have peace. In this world you will have trouble. But take heart! I have overcome the world." (John 16:33) God promises to be with us and to supply us with His inner peace. It is a peace that passes all human understanding.

· · · · · · · · · · · · · · · · · · · · · · · · · · · · · · · · · · · · · · · · · · · · · · · · · · · · · · · · · ·

## Renounce your sinful worry and fill your mind with positive thoughts of our Lord.

· · · · · · · · · · · · · · · · · · · · · · · · · · · · · · · · · · · · · · · · · · · · · · · · · · · · · · · · · ·

Did you hear about the clock that had a nervous breakdown? One day it began thinking about how often it would have to tick in a year. Figuring two ticks a second, 120 a minute, 7,200 an hour, 172,800 a day, and 1,209,600 ticks every week, the clock suddenly realized that it would have to tick nearly 63 million times during the next 12 months. The more it thought about this, the more anxious it became. Finally the clock became so distraught that it suffered a nervous collapse.

Confiding in a clock psychiatrist (a "clock doc"), the clock complained that it didn't have the strength to tick that often. The doctor responded, "But how many ticks must you tick at a time?"

The clock answered, "Only one."

"Well, simply tick one tick at a time and don't worry about the next one," advised the doctor. "You will get along fine, I'm sure."

That's exactly what the clock did, and as is true of all good stories, it ticked happily ever after.

Is there some problem that looks unsolvable to you? Does your burden appear too heavy for you to bear? Does the future seem full of threat to you? Cast your burden on the Lord; ask Him to help you just for today. Renounce your sinful worry and fill your mind with positive thoughts of our Lord.

## TO THINK ABOUT:

- On a scale of 1-5, how much do you worry? (1 – constantly, 5 – rarely) Explain.

- What if you don't feel like rejoicing? What should you do?

- Name someone who rarely appears worried about anything. What is that person like? What do you admire about him or her?

- Why do you think worry is one of the top temptations for many Christians?

- Can you worry and pray at the same time? Explain.

- What are some of your own practical ideas for learning to control your thoughts?

- Why is peace not the same as the absence of problems?


## FOR THE FOLLOWING SCRIPTURES, ASK:
○ What does it say?    ○ What does it mean?    ○ How can you apply it?

- Matthew 6:33-34
- Romans 8:28
- Philippians 4:4-8

# CHAPTER 7

# Dealing with Low Self-Esteem

Many Christians suffer from a sense of low self-worth. They constantly condemn themselves because they do not feel worthy of God's love and forgiveness. Psychiatrist Alfred Adler coined the phrase "inferiority complex" to describe people who feel that they are less acceptable than others.

Low self-esteem usually manifests itself in one of two ways. First, some people withdraw from others. Their lack of self-worth causes them to be shy or introverted. They sit passively on the sidelines as life passes them by. On the other hand, some people express their feelings of inferiority by being brash, loud, and boastful. Their bravado is usually an attempt to cover their feeling of poor self-worth. These people often verbally humiliate others in an attempt to bring them down to their self-perceived level.

Low self-esteem can be especially confusing to Christians because it prevents them from accepting who they are in Christ. We could say they struggle with a "spiritual" inferiority complex.

### Feeling Unworthy of God's Love

In Revelation 12:10, the devil is identified as the "accuser of our brothers" who accuses us before God day and night. It is evident that the devil also whispers accusations in our ears as well, and Christians suffering from low spiritual self-worth actually listen to all he has to say. We must realize that it is natural for us to feel that we are not worthy of God's love. In Luke 15, Jesus told the story of a prodigal son who felt that he could never be worthy of his father's forgiveness and love. After he realized his folly, he said, "I will set out and go back to my father and say to him: Father, I have sinned against heaven and against you. I am no longer worthy to be called your son..." (Luke 15:18-19) In this revealing statement, the prodigal son (who represents us) makes three statements. The first two are correct; however, the third is misleading.

> # We must realize that it is natural for us to feel that we are not worthy of God's love.

First, he admits he has sinned against heaven. That is true. Second, he admits he has sinned against his father. That also is true. However, when he says he is no longer worthy to be called his father's son, he misrepresents his relationship with his father. He assumes that there once was a time when he *was* worthy. However, was he ever worthy to be called a son of his father? Being someone's child is not something that is earned or deserved. It is simply the benefit of being born into a family.

In the same way, we have never been worthy to be called a child of God. Salvation is a gift through the unmerited grace of God.

> Saving is all his idea, and all his work. All we do is trust him enough to let him do it. It's God's gift from start to finish! We don't play the major role. If we did, we'd probably go around bragging that we'd done the whole thing! (Ephesians 2:8-9, The Message)

Instead of insisting that there must be something you have to do or say to make you worthy, realize that His love is completely unconditional. We do not deserve His love; we simply accept it.

### Comparing Yourself to Others

Christians who compare themselves to people who are naturally, intellectually, or physically gifted can also exhibit a sense of inferiority. Since they do not possess these outstanding abilities themselves, they feel that they are of little worth to God. However, when Paul wrote to the church at Corinth, he gave a startling profile of the kind of person that God actually delights to use:

> Brothers, think of what you were when you were called. Not many of you were wise by human standards; not many were influential; not many were of noble birth. But God chose the foolish things of the world to shame the wise; God chose the weak things of the world to shame the strong. He chose the lowly things of this world and the despised things—and the things that are not—to nullify the things that are, so that no one may boast before him. It is because of him that you are in Christ Jesus, who has become for us wisdom from God—that is, our righteousness, holiness and redemption. Therefore, as it is written, "Let him who boasts boast in the Lord." (1 Corinthians 1:26-31)

According to this passage, there are a few gifted people that God can use, but they are definitely in the minority. Let's look at the profiles of some of these unusually gifted people God uses.

........................................................

## Since they do not possess these outstanding abilities themselves, they feel that they are of little worth to God.

........................................................

### Intellectually Gifted

First, God has chosen people who are intellectually gifted, but not many. I am grateful for every intellectual who has faithfully served Christ, like C. S. Lewis and Wernher von Braun. Lewis was professor of Medieval Renaissance Literature at Cambridge University. One of the greatest thinkers of the 20th century, he was an unbeliever who set out to disprove the claims of Christianity in the Bible. In the process of his study, he became a committed Christian who was able to explain theology in terms so simple and clear that they could be captured in a series of children's books called *The Chronicles of Narnia*.

Likewise, Wernher von Braun was a brilliant intellectual who was forced to head Adolph Hitler's rocket program during World War II, although he vehemently opposed the Nazi movement. During the last days of the war, he defected from Germany to America. This ingenious rocket scientist paved the way for America's space program. He lived in Huntsville, Alabama, and directed the development of the rocket program at the Redstone Arsenal. He was a deeply committed Christian who displayed a humble spirit through his faith.

················································································

# If you are not an intellectual, don't fear; you are still a prime candidate to be used by the Lord.

················································································

While there are many other brilliant men and women have served Christ, intellectual giants are a minority in God's army. In fact, sometimes a high I.Q. is a barrier to accepting the simple Gospel with childlike faith. If you are not an intellectual, don't fear; you are still a prime candidate to be used by the Lord.

### People of Influence

According to Paul, God has not called many people of influence to serve Him either. Well known Christians like Billy Graham, Beth Moore, and Max Lucado are familiar names. There are also influential people in society, sports, and Hollywood who are committed Christians—although there aren't many who are willing to make their faith known. For 28 years, Tom Landry coached the Dallas Cowboys and continues to be one of the most well respected celebrities in professional sports even after his death in 2000. He never hesitated to speak of his love for Jesus Christ. In his autobiography he wrote:

> As a Christian I believe my past is forgiven; I can start over with a clean slate. The mistakes of the past need not hold me back. Neither does my fear of failure because as a Christian I believe God is in ultimate control of my life.[19]

We should be thankful for every high-profile person who shares Christ through his or her sphere of influence. But don't let that intimidate you into thinking that God can only use you if you become famous. Christian celebrities are the minority.

## God is not interested in using only those with money or prestige— He chooses people from "upstairs and downstairs" to work for Him.

### People Who Are Socially Acceptable

The third category of God's minority is the word "noble." Paul refers to people who are born into society. When Americans think of nobility, they may envision the popular British television series, *Downton Abbey*, a period drama about the nobility who live upstairs in a huge British estate and the servants who live in the more meager quarters downstairs. God is not interested in using only those with money or prestige—He chooses people from "upstairs and downstairs" to work for Him side-by-side.

---

19 Tom Landry, *An Autobiography* (Grand Rapids, Michigan: Zondervan Publishing House, 1990), p. 294.

Lady Huntington was born into the pinnacle of British nobility.
She accepted Christ during the revival that swept England in the
19th century. She was once asked how she, one of the country's
noble women, had been converted. She replied, "By one letter." She
explained, "In God's Word, 1 Corinthians 1:26, it says, 'Not many
noble are called.' That 'm' saved my soul. For if He had said, '...not
*any* noble,' I would have been lost. So, God bless the little letter 'm'
before 'any' to the salvation of my soul."[20] Are you "someone" in society
because of your name? Be thankful, realizing you are a special minority
on God's team. And don't worry if you're just a "nobody" in social
circles. Jesus' parents were a teenage mother and a village carpenter.

## GOD'S MIGHTY MAJORITY

God can use exceptionally gifted people, but more often than not,
He delights to use simple, everyday folks like you and me. Why?
He receives even greater glory by doing extraordinary things in and
through ordinary people. Paul mentions five specific categories of the
majority of people God uses. You might be surprised at some of the
A-listers here.

· · · · · · · · · · · · · · · · · · · · · · · · · · · · · · · · · · · · · · · · · · ·

Don't worry if you're just a "nobody"
in social circles. Jesus' parents were a
teenage mother and a village carpenter.

· · · · · · · · · · · · · · · · · · · · · · · · · · · · · · · · · · · · · · · · · · ·

### The Foolish

Up first? The foolish. The English word *moron* is derived from a
Greek word that literally means to "be empty-headed." Sometimes
God will bypass a Dr. Dry-as-Dust and instead choose a dedicated,

---

20  Paul Lee Tan, *Signs Of The Times* (Rockville, Maryland: Assurance Publishers, 1979), p. 1232.

but uneducated, backwoods believer to win many souls.

The great evangelist of the 19th century, Dwight L. Moody, is a prime example of how God takes the foolish things of this world to confound the wise. Moody had only a third grade education. He became a Christian when he was seventeen years old. When he presented himself for church membership, the church rejected him because they didn't think he knew enough about Christ. Thankfully, this setback did not deter him. He established a Sunday school class for boys in the inner city of Chicago. He began to teach them to read the Bible. God blessed this effort as the beginning of a ministry that would soon extend worldwide.

## He receives even greater glory by doing extraordinary things in and through ordinary people.

Moody was never ordained and never attended seminary, but the Lord used him mightily. His critics said that he murdered the King's English, noting that he could pronounce the word Jerusalem in only one syllable. (Try that yourself!) Moody was once invited to speak at the respected Cambridge University in England. He stood up and started his address to these highly sophisticated students by saying, "Don't never think that God don't love you, for He do." Although he knew few grammatical rules, he knew the Lord. Many students came to know Christ that day.[21]

Moody also had a problem with stuttering and often had great difficulty speaking. Once when he was preaching a revival, an usher brought a folded note to the platform. Moody opened the note and saw that it only had one word on it: fool. Undaunted by the obvious insult, he said to the audience, "You know, many times I

---

21  William R. Moody, *The Life Of Dwight L. Moody* (New York: H. Revell Company, 1900).

have received letters from people who forgot to sign their names. This is the first letter I've ever gotten where they signed their name and forgot to give the message." Then he quickly changed his text to Psalm 14:1: "The fool says in his heart, 'There is no God …'" On another occasion, a woman criticized him for his poor grammar, saying, "Mr. Moody, you should be ashamed of yourself." He replied, "Dear Lady, I am ashamed of myself, but I'm not ashamed of my Lord Jesus Christ."[22]

· · · · · · · · · · · · · · · · · · · · · · · · · · · · · · · · · · · · · · · · · · · · · · · · · · · ·

# I've heard people excuse themselves from serving Christ because they are too old or too slow.

· · · · · · · · · · · · · · · · · · · · · · · · · · · · · · · · · · · · · · · · · · · · · · · · · · · ·

Moody preached both on this continent and Europe and saw many thousands of people won to Christ. Today Moody Bible Institute and Moody Publishers still carry on his work. During that same time there were many preachers who were more highly educated, but God used Dwight L. Moody, a foolish man according to the world's standards.

### The Weak

Another surprising category of the kind of person God enjoys using is the "weak." God has chosen the weak things of the world to shame the strong. I've heard people excuse themselves from serving Christ because they are too old or too slow. Some have pointed to other physical problems as the reason why they cannot serve. However, it's the very fact that you are weak that God delights to use you.

There are many wonderful examples of how God uses fragile people for His glory. I am always inspired by the story of Fanny

22    Ibid.

Crosby (1820-1915). Although she was blind, she was perhaps the most prolific hymn writer our nation has ever known. Her life began with an unfortunate tragedy at the age of six months when she developed a painful eye inflammation and her physician inadvertently put the wrong medicine in her eyes. Instead of treating her condition, it caused her to become totally blind.

......................................................................

# Stop using your physical disabilities or weaknesses as an excuse for not serving the Lord.

......................................................................

Those were the days before people turned suing for malpractice into a multi-billion dollar industry. Years later, when asked if she was bitter about the fact that her physician caused her to be blind, she replied, "If I could meet that doctor now, I would say thank you, thank you, over and over again, for making me blind. I could not have written thousands of hymns if I had been hindered by the distractions of seeing all the interesting and beautiful objects that would have been presented to my notice."[23] Fanny Crosby wrote over 8,000 hymns, including *To God Be the Glory*, and *Blessed Assurance, Jesus Is Mine*. If God can use a blind person to write music, God can certainly use you. Stop using your physical disabilities or weaknesses as an excuse for not serving the Lord.

### The Lowly

A lowly person is the opposite of nobility. However, someone who is born without a pedigree or someone who is born into a broken and troubled family situation has the potential for a great testimony of God's grace. If you did not come from a Christian home, people

---

23 Warren W. Wiersbe, *Victorious Christians You Should Know* (Grand Rapids, Michigan: Baker Book House, 1984), p. 23.

who have been blessed with the heritage of a Christian family may intimidate you. You may be embarrassed that there aren't more Christians in your family. Your parents may be divorced. Or maybe you are the one who is divorced. Don't fret; God can still use you.

••••••••••••••••••••••••••••••••••••••••••••••••••••••••••••••••••••••••

# Have you noticed that the world naturally despises anything labeled "Christian"?

••••••••••••••••••••••••••••••••••••••••••••••••••••••••••••••••••••••••

Another one of my heroines of the faith is Ethel Waters, a committed Christian who sang for many years on the Billy Graham crusade team. I once heard her share the poignant details of her life and testimony at one of their crusades. She had to overcome the shame of being born as the consequence of incest. However, she could stand up in front of thousands of people and say with a smile, "God don't make no junk." When she sang, "His eye is on the sparrow, and I know He watches me," you could see the love of Jesus Christ radiating from her face. If God can use a wonderful Christian lady like Ethel Waters, who was of ignoble birth, He can certainly use you.

## The Despised

This refers to people the world shrugs off and considers of no importance. Others may even laugh at them and ridicule them. Have you noticed that the world naturally despises anything labeled "Christian"? When it comes to money, promotion, publicity, buildings, and finances, the world definitely outclasses the Church. For example, there are many more Christian movies making their way into mainstream media today. They don't have big Hollywood budgets, but they are still making an impact with their growing popularity. However, I always smile when I see how many professional movie critics utterly disregard Christian-themed movies when they hit the theaters. It's as if they cannot bring themselves to positively review a movie with a redemptive premise. However, God uses what is often ridiculed so that He may receive more glory.

### The Ignored

Paul says that God chose to use "the things that are not." (1 Corinthians 1:28) Do you feel that others overlook you or leave you out entirely? As if you are not even there? You may not believe it, but you're in good company if you feel a little ignored. One of the little known nobodies who had a powerful impact on the kingdom of God was Edward Kimball. Chances are, you have never heard of this man. However, Kimball led Dwight L. Moody to Christ. On April 21, 1855, Kimball went into a Chicago shoe store where Moody sold shoes and engaged Moody in a spiritual conversation. Although his name is largely unknown today, Kimball's personal witness helped produce one of history's greatest evangelists.[24]

> However, God uses what is often ridiculed so that He may receive more glory.

The trail of influence extends even further as Moody later had a tremendous influence on the life of F. B. Meyer (1847-1929), a British Baptist pastor and author of many Christian books. While Meyer was preaching in America, he then encouraged a young seminary student by the name of Wilbur Chapman to be faithful to his calling. Chapman was an effective evangelist for many years. He eventually turned over his evangelistic ministry to a young ex-baseball player by the name of Billy Sunday. For the first two decades of the 20th Century, Billy Sunday was the most popular and celebrated preacher in America and reached thousands of people

---

24  Warren W. Wiersbe, *Be Mature* (Wheaton, Illinois: Victor Books, 1979), p. 93.

for Christ. Amazingly, one of the people who became a Christian in one of Billy Sunday's campaigns was Billy Graham's father, Frank Graham.[25] Without the witness of God's "nobody," Edward Kimball, who knows whether or not Billy Graham would have become the most influential evangelist in modern history?

## FULLY SURRENDER YOUR LIFE TO GOD

God can do mighty things through every life that is surrendered to Him. First Corinthians 1:29 explains why God uses people who are not naturally gifted: "…so that no one may boast before him…" In other words, He wants it to be obvious that Jesus gets all the credit for whatever God accomplishes through a person.

............................................................

# You cannot stand before God on the basis of your own goodness. No one can.

............................................................

Paul goes on to write in verse 30: "It is because of him that you are in Christ Jesus, who has become for us wisdom from God—that is, our righteousness, holiness and redemption." Jesus is everything we need for a healthy self-esteem. You cannot stand before God on the basis of your own goodness. No one can. According to Isaiah 64:6, "…our righteous acts are like filthy rags." Jesus represents us through His righteousness. If you are His, God looks at you right now—with all your faults fully known to Him—and He calls you holy because He sees you through the filter of the perfect righteousness of His Son. You don't have to strain and struggle to be holy before God because you are covered by the holiness of Jesus Christ.

---

25   Adrian P. Rogers, *Mastering Your Emotions* (Nashville, Tennessee: Broadman Press, 1988), p. 79.

So if you struggle with a feeling of low self-esteem, realize that you are somebody special because of God's love for you. A very wise preacher once told me, "God doesn't love you because you are valuable. You are valuable because God loves you."

During this life, you will find that there are many places where you will not be accepted. There may be organizations that will not accept you for membership. Certain circles of people may reject you. But you can rejoice because God Himself has fully embraced you just the way you are. Leave your feelings of low self-esteem behind. Instead, remind yourself at the beginning of each day: "Through Jesus Christ, I am somebody special to God. Because He loves me, I can love myself."

......................................................................

## You don't have to strain and struggle to be holy before God because you are covered by the holiness of Jesus Christ.

......................................................................

## TO THINK ABOUT:

- What causes a person to feel unworthy of God's love?

- What was the most surprising characteristic of "God's Mighty Majority"?

- How does God redeem our mistakes for our good and the good of others?

- When was a time God used your weaknesses to give Himself more glory?

- How would you describe "who you are in Christ" as a result of God's love? List all the descriptive words that come to mind.

- Who taught you by example what unconditional love is?

- What holds people back from fully surrendering to God? What does a fully surrendered Christian look like?

## FOR THE FOLLOWING SCRIPTURES, ASK:

O What does it say?    O What does it mean?    O How can you apply it?

- Isaiah 43:1-4
- 1 Corinthians 1:26-31
- Ephesians 5:1-2

# CHAPTER 8

# All Stressed Up and No Place to Go

When I first published this book in 1993, one out of every five Americans struggled with hypertension. However, today's numbers are staggering. The Centers for Disease Control and Prevention now states that one out of three Americans has high blood pressure.[26] If two of your neighbors seem okay to you, I guess you're the one who should worry!

Many who go to physicians are there primarily because of stress-related problems. According to the National Institutes of Health, the consequences of too much stress can manifest in digestive problems, headaches, sleeplessness, depressed mood, anger, and irritability.[27] It can literally make you sick, too. Those who are "under chronic stress" get more frequent and severe viral infections, such as the flu or common cold. The NIH also indicates that vaccines, such as the flu shot, are less effective for those who experience chronic stress.[28]

## DEALING WITH STRESS

We spend billions of dollars each year to lower our stress level. Unfortunately, in most cases, suffering people are merely treating external symptoms, rather than the internal cause of stress.

---

26  Centers for Disease Control and Prevention website, http://www.cdc.gov/bloodpressure/facts. htm, accessed August 24, 2014.

27  National Institutes of Health website, http://www.nlm.nih.gov/medlineplus/stress.html, accessed August 24, 2014.

28  Ibid.

The concept of "stress" relates to pressure applied either from outside or from within. Stress is a term familiar not only in psychology but also in engineering and architecture as well. When an architect designs a building, he is careful to calculate the stress-bearing capacity of the wall and roof. He designs load-bearing walls to bear much more than the actual weight of the roof of the building. He also calculates the effect of wind, snow, and ice. Careful architects utilize a formula that allows a generous margin of safety.

## We perform best when we are under an acceptable level of pressure.

The Divine Designer, God our Father, created us with a capacity to bear stress, as it is part of life. The psalmist describes God's intimate familiarity with our personality this way: "He knows us inside and out." (Psalm 103:14, The Message). As the Heavenly Architect, our Creator understands how much stress and pressure we can withstand. The English word *stress* is derived from the Latin word *strictus*, which means, "to be drawn tight." The French word *estresse* means, "narrowness or tightness." These are apt descriptions of what stress does to us. Consider the relationship between a rubber band and stress. A rubber band under no tension is loose and worthless. Remember, a person who manages to experience no stress is usually ineffective. A rubber band is designed to function under tension. We perform best when we are under an acceptable level of pressure.

Not all stress is bad. For example, the pressure of a deadline may motivate us to complete our homework or an assignment at work. You may be like the college student who said, "I don't work best under pressure. I work only under pressure." We meet trouble when, like a rubber band, we are stretched to the breaking point. Stress becomes distress when we subject ourselves to continual and extreme pressure. We stretch beyond our designed capacity. Just as a rubber band may break, we also may experience breakdown.

In order to cope with stress effectively, we must make three realizations:

**(1) Stress is an unavoidable part of our existence.**
If you are searching for a stress-free existence, forget it! It is impossible to avoid all stress in life. Stress is naturally associated with any type of activity or relationship. The only way to avoid it would be to never do anything or never associate with anyone. To compare it to baseball, this would be like living a life consisting of no runs, no hits, and no errors. Stress is one of the natural price tags attached to life.

**(2) We have an optimal stress level.**
This is the point at which stress motivates us to do our very best. When we operate at our optimal stress level, our lives will be dynamic, purposeful, and happy. To exceed that stress level is to risk a breakdown. However, to live too far under the level is to muddle through life as an underachiever, never attaining our God-given potential.

**(3) We can have excessive stress in life.**
Dr. Lloyd J. Ogilvie identifies five of the most common causes of stress: change, conflict, criticism, concerns, and crises.[29] Are any of these major stress-producing factors present in your life now? Are you carrying so much stress that you are approaching the breaking point? Have you crossed the line between your optimal stress level and distress?

---

29   Dr. Lloyd J. Ogilvie, *Making Stress Work For You* (Waco, Texas: Word Books, 1984), p. 37.

## SOURCES OF EXCESSIVE STRESS

In Levelland, Texas, John Yates received his lost dog after he put this ad in the paper: "Lost or strayed, Chihuahua, answering to name of Chico. Brilliant dog, acutely aware of national and world politics— he shakes all the time."[30] Let's face it—we live in a stressful world. Excessive, continual stress can be damaging to your emotional and physical health. The following are some specific symptoms that will help you identify the presence of critical stress.

*Physical Stress*
     The late Dr. Hans Selye was recognized early on as the most imminent authority on stress and pioneered research into how stress affects us physically. When we are subjected to stress, a complex part of our brain and body called the autonomic nervous system kicks in to prepare us to deal with the stressful challenge. This is often called the "fight-or-flight" response. Stress is part of this vital warning system of endorphins and hormones that God has given us to enable us to know what to do in a dangerous situation. Our body automatically shifts into overdrive to either deal with the threat or run from it. A small part of our brain called the hypothalamus releases neurotransmitters, which in turn stimulate the release of hormones. The most common hormone is adrenaline. When you are under the sudden stress of getting a bad phone call from your boss, for example, you can easily feel this "adrenaline rush."
     Consider the following symptoms of stress and see if you can identify these from your personal experience:[31]

> First, your digestive system slows down so that blood
> may be redirected to your muscles and brain. Your body
> determines that it is more important to be alert in the
> face of danger than to digest your food. *Have you ever felt
> "butterflies in your stomach"?*

---

30   Paul Lee Tan, *Signs Of The Times* (Rockville, Maryland: Assurance Publishers, 1979), p. 1448.

31   Edward E. Charlesworth and Ronald G. Nathan, *Stress Management* (New York: Ballantine Books, 1982), pp. 4-9.

During stress, your respiration automatically increases to send more oxygen to your muscles. *How long does it take you to catch your breath after facing a threat?*

Your heart starts pumping faster, and your blood pressure rises to force blood to all the parts of your body. *Have you ever thought you could hear your heart pounding in your ears?*

Perspiration also increases to cool your body. This allows you to burn more energy in a shorter period of time. *Have you ever sweated through your shirt before a presentation at work?*

During stress, your muscles become tense in preparation for action. *Have you ever complained of a stiff back or neck after a particularly stressful day?*

Under stress, sugar and fats pour into your blood to supply fuel for quick energy. The corresponding release of adrenaline often allows people to accomplish almost supernatural feats of strength. We have all heard stories of a mother pulling a car off of an injured child due to the release of adrenaline. *Have you ever jumped four feet straight in the air the minute you almost stepped on a snake?*

Even the Lord Jesus was not immune to the physical symptoms of excessive stress. The physician, Luke, tells us that Jesus was in such anguish in Gethsemane that "his sweat was like drops of blood falling to the ground." (Luke 22:44) As Jesus faced the betrayal, denial, and the prospect of an agonizing death, He was subjected to tremendous pressure. He told His disciples, "My soul is overwhelmed with sorrow to the point of death." (Mark 14:34)

### Emotional Stress

In addition to these various physical symptoms, there are emotional symptoms of stress as well. However, these are harder to recognize. Most of us have endured the unpleasant experience of sitting all day with a loved one in a hospital room. This labor of love doesn't drain us physically, but somehow we are emotionally exhausted at the end of the day. Stress will sap our emotional energy faster than physical labor. We tend to deny what our emotions are telling us. Have you ever come home after an unusually stressful day at the office feeling irritable? We usually pass our irritability along to those around us. Stress can damage our relationships as it ripples from person to person.

........................................................................

# Pronounced stress can produce depression and a sense of hopelessness and helplessness.

........................................................................

While it may be possible to bounce back from a bad day, the effects of ongoing stress can be devastating. Under the pressure of long-term stress, our personality may actually change. Pronounced stress can produce depression and a sense of hopelessness and helplessness. We may become tense and explosive in our responses to loved ones and even strangers.

The Holmes and Rahe Stress Scale is a scale of 43 highly stressful events that can lead to illness. It was developed in 1967 by psychiatrists Thomas Holmes and Richard Rahe and assigns points to events that have occurred in the past year of an individual to give a rough estimate of how stress can affect health. The strongest stress-producing event is the death of a spouse, followed by the death of someone in your immediate family. The second most stress-producing event is divorce, followed by marital separation. Other top stress producers are: the loss of a job, major surgery, the birth of a child, getting married, a child leaving home, retiring, changing jobs, or moving to a new city. Have you gone through or are you going through any of these stress-producing events? Notice that not all of these events are negative, but they still produce stress. Take a moment to gaze into your emotional mirror and see if you are suffering from the emotional sources and symptoms of stress.

## PRACTICAL STEPS TO REDUCE STRESS

Once you recognize the sources and symptoms of excessive stress in your life, then you are able to move on to take steps to reduce that stress. In *The Neurotic Personality*, Karen Harvey discusses four ways that people deal with excessive stress. First, some people simply *Deny* the presence of prolonged stress, hoping their symptoms will magically go away. Second, some people simply try to *Rationalize* it by saying that everyone is stressed out. They are no different from their neighbor, so what's the big deal? Third, many people *Narcoticize* their stress. In 2011, almost 49 million prescriptions were written for the anti-anxiety drug, Xanax. Fourth, some people simply try to *Avoid* all stress-producing experiences.

Have you been trying to deal with your stress in one of these ways? I believe the best way to handle stress is not by denying, rationalizing, narcotizing, or avoiding it. The most effective way to deal with stress is to work to reduce stress to an acceptable level. Let me suggest five practical steps you can take:

1.  **Learn to relax your body.**
    Even the most stressed-out person can learn to relax. Try it right now. One by one, begin to intentionally relax each part of your body. Start with your toes and move up to your neck. Now, take several deep breaths. Feel any better?

    I am aware that the reason some people go to sleep in church is that it is the only time during the week that they are still, quiet, and relaxed. I tell my congregation that if the only thing they get out of my sermon is a 20-minute nap, at least they got something out of it!

2.  **Learn to relax your mind.**
    The famous cardiologist Robert Elliott said, "To avoid stress, rule number one is, don't sweat the small stuff. Rule number two is, all stuff is small stuff. And if you can't fight and you can't flee, flow."[32] Once you recognize that

---

32   Quoted by Lloyd Cory, *Quotable Quotations* (Wheaton: Victor Books, 1985), p. 369.

every threat is relatively insignificant when viewed from an external perspective, you are able to relax. Like relaxing your muscles, relaxing your mind takes a conscious effort.

Throughout a stressful day, you should schedule brief one-minute mental vacations when you tune out everything and park your mind in neutral. Try one right now. After you read this paragraph, close your eyes, breathe in deeply through your nose and exhale slowly through your mouth. Imagine yourself blowing all your cares out as you exhale. Concentrate only on your breathing. Do this for 12 breaths, counting slowly as you exhale.

Try planning these mental vacations during times of stress. (Of course, never try it while you're driving, and don't plan them too often or you will stay tuned out!) As you learn to schedule these brief moments of quiet, you'll find that Christ can renew your mind and settle your thoughts.

3. **Learn to laugh more.**
   Laughter relaxes us as almost nothing else can. Emotionally healthy people have learned to laugh at themselves. They understand that they do not have to take themselves seriously in order to take life seriously. They recognize that any day above ground is a good one.

   Life is 10 percent how you make it and 90 percent how you take it. If you can laugh at it, you can generally live with it. A cheerful lady once shared with me, "Laughter that is suppressed goes down and spreads to your hips." So, go ahead and laugh—don't hold it in.

4. **Don't carry your burdens alone.**
   Find someone with whom you can share your deepest problems. Talk to your spouse, parents, counselor, or pastor. Find a group of friends with whom you can be honest and transparent. Men are especially reticent about discussing their problems. They tend to internalize their problems until their issues develop into ulcers. Many men are like a

duck on a pond. Above the surface, everything looks calm and collected, but below the surface the duck is paddling like crazy. I know many men who appear calm, but a storm is raging on the inside. Open up your heart and share your problems with others.

When I was in my early thirties, I was carrying more stress than I could carry alone. I was finishing my doctorate, while pastoring a church with over a thousand members. My mother was also living with us because she was in the last stages of cancer, and I was taking her for regular chemotherapy treatments. At the same time, a much larger church was talking to me about becoming their pastor. Stress was stretching my "rubber band" dangerously tight.

........................................................................

## Life is 10 percent how you make it and 90 percent how you take it. If you can laugh at it, you can generally live with it.

........................................................................

I thought I was handling it well until I noticed that I was losing weight (without trying). I found it harder to sleep at night. Stress was affecting me physically and emotionally. I was outwardly calm, but I was a mess inside. Fortunately, I was part of a discipleship group of committed Christians. They recognized that I was hurting and lovingly drew me out of my isolation. At first I didn't want to talk about my problems. I had been denying my feelings while trying as a pastor to help other people who were hurting. These friends tenderly but persistently prodded me to the point where I could unload my burden with them. One afternoon, I cried as I shared my feelings, fears, and anxiety. As they hugged me and prayed with me, I experienced a deep sense of relief. Can you think of a person or group with whom you may share your burdens?

## EXCHANGE YOUR STRESS FOR GOD'S STRENGTH

So far, you could get my suggestions on reducing stress from any secular psychologist. Any non-believer could recommend that you relax your mind and body, laugh more, and share your burdens. However, Christians can enjoy an added dimension of strength from God to lighten their load. God's stress-reducing instructions are found in the Old Testament book of Isaiah:

> Do you not know? Have you not heard? The Lord is the everlasting God, the Creator of the ends of the earth. He will not grow tired or weary, and his understanding no one can fathom. He gives strength to the weary and increases the power of the weak. Even youths grow tired and weary, and young men stumble and fall; but those who hope in the Lord will renew their strength. They will soar on wings like eagles; they will run and not grow weary, they will walk and not be faint. (Isaiah 40:28-31)

Verse 31 says, "…they that wait upon the Lord shall renew their strength." (KJV) The key to this promise is the word *renew*. The Hebrew word *chaleth* literally means, "to exchange." According to this passage, we may exchange our stress for His strength and learn to wait, soar, run, and walk.

················································································

When you possess a servant's heart and are willing to do whatever God asks, your stress level will decrease.

················································································

### Wait—on the Lord

If I offered to exchange a $100 bill for your $1 bill, you would be foolish not to agree. This passage in Isaiah promises a better trade than that. You may come to God with your weakness and stress and exchange it for His supernatural strength. "Waiting on the Lord" doesn't mean that we sit passively and do nothing. "Waiting on the Lord" is a picture of a servant waiting on his master like a waiter or waitress in a restaurant. When you possess a servant's heart and are willing to do whatever God asks, your stress level will decrease. As we seek the Lord daily, He supplies our strength. I have found the best method of reducing stress is to seek God during a daily quiet time before we meet the day's demands. God promises to supply us with strength if we will seek Him each day with a servant's heart.

### Soar–Like an Eagle

God also promises strength to soar like an eagle. Perhaps you have faced times of intense difficulty when your problems churned in waves of adversity. An eagle doesn't fly away from a storm; it actually flies toward it. During a storm, it can fly the highest and the fastest on powerful updrafts that take the eagle far above the storm. Can you claim that kind of soaring ability during times of great trouble? God says you may possess it when you turn to Him for strength.

### Run–with Patience

God also supplies us strength to run and not grow weary. When you face pressures and problems that demand your patience in order to manage them, God supplies supernatural power to prevent weariness and burnout. We all face deadlines. Someone said, "They call them deadlines because they kill you to meet them." The Christian life is not a 100-meter dash; it is a lifetime marathon that demands the patience and pacing of God. Stress does not last forever. If you feel like quitting, pace yourself and do not give up. The finish line is near.

### Walk–with Confidence

Finally, God promises to supply the ability to walk with confidence. Consider the order of these three promises when we wait on God: (1) Strength to soar like an eagle; (2) Strength to run with patience; (3) Strength to walk with confidence. For many years, I thought God had listed these in descending order of importance. Surely soaring like an eagle is harder than walking and not fainting. However, I have come to understand that God listed these promises in a mighty crescendo of truth. There are only a few times in our lives when we are required to soar like an eagle; however, we need strength to walk each day. Walking daily in the Spirit is not anti-climatic—it is the ultimate evidence of supernatural strength. I admit that I need the greatest strength simply to be a good father and husband. We need strength to carry out the daily, mundane requirements of our lives. It is often a greater miracle to "walk and not faint" than it is to soar like an eagle.

In this chapter, we've learned that stress can make us stronger when we turn to God and surrender to Him. Don't be all stressed up with no place to go; you do have somewhere to turn. Go to God and wait on Him, serving Him with all your heart.

## TO THINK ABOUT:

- How do you typically deal with stress?

- What stressful events/situations have you encountered in the past six months (change, conflict, criticism, concerns, or crises) that might be affecting your health?

- What is your "optimal stress level"? Are you at that level right now, or have you exceeded it?

- What physical symptoms do you experience when you are stressed?

- What emotional symptoms do you experience when you are stressed?

- Of the four stress-busters mentioned (relaxing your body, relaxing your mind, laughing more, and sharing your burdens), which are the easiest for you to practice? Which are the most difficult? Why?

- Sometimes we're doing well just to "walk and not faint." What advice would you have for someone who is barely hanging on because of stress?

## FOR THE FOLLOWING SCRIPTURES, ASK:
○ What does it say?    ○ What does it mean?    ○ How can you apply it?

- Psalm 36:5-6
- Psalm 105:4
- Isaiah 40:28-31

# CHAPTER 9

# The Little Foxes of Frustration

In the chapter on stress, we examined some of the major stress-producing experiences of life, including the death of a spouse or family member, divorce, losing a job, or other traumatic events. However, there is another extreme that can also damage us emotionally: the insignificant frustrations of life that wear us down. We tend to ignore these daily frustrations until they begin to add up to one big problem.

In my personal life, I have usually been able to deal with a major crisis easier than with minor inconveniences. When both of my parents were dying of cancer, I realized that I needed to walk more closely with the Lord to endure the stress. I knew I could not survive that kind of pressure without the supernatural power of God and the caring support of other Christians.

However, I must confess that a flat tire or missed connection at the airport had the potential to bug me more than some of life's larger issues. As I've grown older, and hopefully a little wiser, I've learned not to let these inconsequential events bother me. However, we all share this tendency to trip over the "little things."

## WHAT DOES IT TAKE TO FRUSTRATE YOU?

Methodist evangelist, Sam Jones, once wrote, "I don't mind being swallowed by a whale, but I hate to be nibbled to death by a bunch of minnows."[33] Most of us are better equipped to deal with the big problems of life, but we may stumble over something as inconsequential as someone ahead of us in line taking too long in the drive-through at our favorite fast food place.

·············································································

# We must be on guard against the "little foxes" of frustration that creep into our lives and rob us of fruitfulness.

·············································································

There is an obscure but profound verse of scripture hidden in the beautiful little book, Song of Solomon. This Old Testament book is a passionate love poem describing the romance of a man and woman. It also vividly depicts the mystic love between Christ and His church. In the story, the handsome prince wants to take away the beautiful young girl he has discovered working in the vineyard. She wants to go, but she politely refuses because she is assigned to guard the vineyard. In Song of Solomon 2:15 she says, "Catch for us the foxes, the little foxes that ruin the vineyards, our vineyards that are in bloom." In ancient Israel, miniature foxes often damaged the fragile blossoms on the vines, leaving no potential for fruit. The young maiden was there to guard against these little foxes that could create great problems.

We must be on guard against the "little foxes" of frustration that creep into our lives and rob us of fruitfulness. God's will for your life is that you should bear much fruit. Jesus said, "This is to my Father's glory, that you bear much fruit, showing yourselves to be my disciples." (John 15:8) Minor setbacks curtail our ability to bear the fruit of the Spirit. These are demonic destroyers sent from the devil to keep us spiritually barren.

---

33  George R. Stuart, *Famous Stories of Sam P. Jones* (New York: Fleming H. Revel, Co., 1908), p. 111.

Little things really do count. The French philosopher Montaigne wrote:

> Life is a tender thing and is easily molested. There is always something that goes amiss. Vain vexations—vain sometimes, but always vexatious. The smallest and lightest impediments are the most piercing; and as little letters tire the eyes, so do little affairs most disturb us.[34]

Chances are, you are not disturbed by the sound of a jet taking off overhead. However, if you have ever tried to sleep when a tiny mosquito is buzzing around your ears, you realize that little things irritate the most. The Bible is filled with people who had to deal with frustration. One of the best examples is Nehemiah. God called Nehemiah to the great work of rebuilding the wall around Jerusalem. For many years, he struggled with a never-ending variety of inconveniences. Let's look at four little foxes of frustration that Nehemiah fought that we still face today. These foxes attack our spiritual fruitfulness. If we can successfully identify and combat our own little foxes of frustration, we can enjoy a much more productive life.

......................................................................

## If we can successfully identify and combat our own little foxes of frustration, we can enjoy a much more productive life.

......................................................................

---

34 Quoted by Lloyd Cory, *Quotable Quotations* (Wheaton, Illinois: Victor Books, 1985), p. 149.

## UNPLEASANT AGGRAVATIONS

We must all deal with aggravations and irritations that annoy us. When Nehemiah first attempted to rebuild the wall around Jerusalem, the people were unable to work because they were surrounded by junk after decades of neglect. The people complained, "The strength of the laborers is giving out, and there is so much rubble that we cannot rebuild the wall." (Nehemiah 4:10)

We become tired and frustrated when rubble piles up around us. In his book, *Ordering Your Private World*, Gordon McDonald lists some symptoms of a disorganized life. He states that when every horizontal surface in the path of your life becomes littered, it is a sure sign of disorganization. This may include your desk, bedroom dresser, kitchen counter, or work bench. When your car is dirty inside and out, it may reveal that you are letting rubble pile up in your life.[35]

·················································································

# We must all deal with aggravations and irritations that annoy us.

·················································································

I recently asked some people in my church about the "junk" that aggravates them the most. Perhaps you can relate to some of the answers:

- A husband who continually clicks through the television channels with the remote control
- When someone calls and tries to sell something over the phone
- Call waiting
- People who call and start the conversation by saying, "Guess who this is?"
- Store clerks who pressure you to buy
- People who park in handicapped parking places, but aren't

---

35  Gordon McDonald, *Ordering Your Private World* (Nashville, Tennessee: Thomas Nelson Publishers, 1984), p. 66.

handicapped
- When people get in the express line at the grocery store but have more than 12 items
- People who have their turn signal on and aren't turning
- People who turn without using their turn signal
- Drivers who pass you on the interstate and then slow down in front of you
- Women who put their makeup on in their car
- Husbands who never stop and ask for directions when they are lost

You could add your own suggestions to these aggravations. These unpleasant irritations pile up and can steal our effectiveness in an ordinary day.

## UNFINISHED BUSINESS

A dear friend of mine once gave me a humorous needlepoint, which read, "Finish what you star." How many projects have you started that are still unfinished? Perhaps you started redecorating a room and stopped halfway. Now whenever you walk through the room you are reminded of your unfinished business. Maybe you started an outdoor project like landscaping your yard, and it still has not been completed. Unfinished business is a source of continual pressure.

....................................................................

These unpleasant irritations
pile up and can steal our effectiveness
in an ordinary day.

....................................................................

Zerubbabel, one of Nehemiah's contemporaries, started to rebuild the Jewish Temple with great enthusiasm, but he had to stop when it was only partially completed. For 16 years, no one worked on it. I imagine that every time he looked at the halfway-completed job, he experienced the frustration of unfinished business.

Jesus talked about the importance of finishing what we start. He said, "I have brought you glory by completing the work you gave me to do." (John 17:4) Jesus had a clear understanding of what His Father wanted Him to accomplish. He refused to be sidetracked or distracted. Even as He was hanging on the cross, He said with a sense of fulfillment, "It is finished!" as He completed His task

. . . . . . . . . . . . . . . . . . . . . . . . . . . . . . . . . . . . . . . . . . . . . . . . . . . . . . . . . . . . . . . . . . . . .

## The little foxes of unfinished business will nip at you until you commit yourself to finish those jobs.

. . . . . . . . . . . . . . . . . . . . . . . . . . . . . . . . . . . . . . . . . . . . . . . . . . . . . . . . . . . . . . . . . . . . .

Don't you feel good when you start a project and complete it? Take a moment to survey your life. Are there any unfinished projects or jobs that you need to finish? The little foxes of unfinished business will nip at you until you commit yourself to finish those jobs. The easiest time to become frustrated is halfway through a task. We usually begin a new project with enthusiasm and end with a sense of excitement as we finish it. Halfway through the job is when we are easily discouraged. This is even true of marriage. I don't know of many marriages that fell apart in the first month. However, somewhere in the middle of a marriage that is committed to the long-term, problems can arise. Somewhere between the "I do" and the "You'd better" is where people encounter issues.

## UNDUE CRITICISM

When the Jews resumed their task of rebuilding Jerusalem, they constantly faced the caustic criticism of other people. When their enemies heard that the Jews were rebuilding the wall, the Bible says they responded with opposition. "They all plotted together to come and fight against Jerusalem and stir up trouble against it."

(Nehemiah 4:8) They were involved in a great work, and yet they faced the constant nuisance of undeserved criticism.

You can be sure that when you are attempting a great work for God, you can expect criticism. The door of opportunity always swings upon the hinges of opposition. How should we respond? In Matthew 5:11-12, Jesus gives us the correct response, "Blessed are you when men insult you, persecute you and falsely say all kinds of evil against you because of me. Rejoice and be glad, because great is your reward in heaven, for in the same way they persecuted the prophets who were before you." Jesus encourages us to rejoice and be exceedingly glad when we face this kind of criticism. That's a lot easier to say than to do.

......................................................................

## You can be sure that when you are attempting a great work for God, you can expect criticism.

......................................................................

How many people can read a scathing letter or listen to a vitriolic attack upon their character and respond by smiling and saying, "Praise the Lord, I really enjoyed that!"? It goes against our basic nature. One secret to dealing with criticism is to look for something positive in every critical comment. If you look hard enough, you can usually find a kernel of truth buried in the strongest and even the most obnoxious criticism. Abraham Lincoln might have broken under the strain of his office if he hadn't learned the skill of dealing with unjust criticism. His description of how he handled his critics has become a classic. Even General Douglas MacArthur kept a copy of Lincoln's words hanging above his desk. Winston Churchill also kept a framed copy of these words in his study. Lincoln wrote:

> If I were to try to read, much less to answer all the attacks made on me, this shop might as well be closed for any other business. I do the best I know how—the very best I

can; and I mean to keep on doing so until the end. If the end brings me out alright, then what is said against me won't matter. If the end brings me out wrong, then ten angels swearing I was right would make no difference.[36]

I have a friend who is a pastor of a large church. Several years ago, he made a commitment to rejoice when he was criticized and to look for something positive in every bit of criticism. One day he received an abusive letter from a woman in his church, unmerciful in her angry condemnation. After reading the letter, he had a difficult time trying to derive something positive from it. Then suddenly a wonderful thought came to his mind that allowed him to rejoice. He paused and prayed with a smile on his face, "Lord, I rejoice that at least I am not married to her."

## UNEXPECTED DELAY

Nehemiah had hoped to be able to rebuild the wall as quickly as possible. Opposition and criticism caused a series of unexpected delays. (Anyone who has built a house can relate to that.) But persistence has its own reward, and the Jewish people finally finished the wall. (Nehemiah 6:15) Are you the kind of person who hates to wait? Are you bothered by the fact that all the traffic lights are green until you are running late and every light suddenly changes to red just as you arrive?

••••••••••••••••••••••••••••••••••••••••••••••••••••

But persistence has its own reward, and the Jewish people finally finished the wall. (Nehemiah 6:15)

••••••••••••••••••••••••••••••••••••••••••••••••••••

I tend to be highly motivated to always be on time or usually early. While punctuality is a virtue, we must be careful not to let

36  Dale Carnegie, *How To Enjoy Your Life And Your Job* (New York: Pocket Books, 1970), p. 55.

unexpected delays frustrate us. I recall several years ago I had an extremely busy day scheduled. My day started by driving 40 miles into Birmingham, Alabama, to visit several hospitals where members of the church I pastored had been admitted. I arrived early at one of the hospitals and parked my car in the garage. After making my visit, I returned to my car to discover that I had locked my keys inside.

I searched in vain for someone to help, but there was no one around. I could feel frustration beginning to eat away at me as I considered all the things I had to do that day. Since this happened before the advent of cellphones, I returned to the hospital and called back to the church. Our Minister of Music, Tommy Pierce, was more than willing to go by my house, pick up an extra set of keys and drive them all the way to me.

I returned to the parking garage to wait for his arrival. After waiting for about 10 minutes, a security guard drove up and inquired about my predicament. When I reported that my keys were locked inside, he produced a tool and in a matter of seconds had unlocked the door. I thanked him for his help and waved as he drove off.

......................................................................

## While punctuality is a virtue, we must be careful not to let unexpected delays frustrate us.

......................................................................

My problem was still not solved. Tommy was somewhere on the road to bring me the keys. I couldn't just drive off, and there was no way to get him a message. I wondered what I would say when he got there. I don't know what you would have done in my situation, but after thinking about it for a few moments I put my keys back in the ignition, locked the door, and closed it! I stood waiting for Tommy to get there with the extra keys. When he arrived, I expressed my appreciation for his good deed. To this day he doesn't know the full story (unless he reads this book).

Jesus can teach us something about how to deal with delay. In John 11, we read the story of Jesus' response to Mary and Martha when they sent word that their brother Lazarus was sick. They had expected Jesus to drop everything and rush to the bedside of their dying brother. Instead Jesus deliberately delayed for two days. Finally, when Lazarus had died, Jesus made His appearance in Bethany. Martha was distraught and cried out, "Lord, if you had been here, my brother would not have died." (John 11:21) One can easily detect the underlying question, "What took you so long?" For several days, I imagine Mary and Martha had been pacing the floor, wringing their hands, and wondering where Jesus could be.

······································································

# Other times you pray and both you and the request are right, but the timing is not right.

······································································

Have you ever faced a difficult problem or need in your life, but it seemed as if God did not respond when you called on Him? Like Martha you wanted to say, "God, where were you? I needed you." But heaven seemed to be silent. We must remember that God is never in a hurry. With God, timing is more important than time. God has no wristwatch to constantly consult. He is the Creator of time. "With the Lord a day is like a thousand years, and a thousand years are like a day." (2 Peter 3:8) The reason Jesus delayed in responding to the call of Mary and Martha would soon become obvious when Jesus raised Lazarus from the dead. He had deliberately delayed so that God would receive greater glory from this miracle.

When you pray and the request is not right, God simply says, "No." When you pray and your heart is not right, God says, "Grow." Other times you pray and both you and the request are right, but the timing is not right. God teaches us the discipline of delay by saying, "Slow." He is going to answer you, but He will do so in His own time. However, when you pray and the timing, requests, and your heart are right, God responds by saying, "Go!"

## DISCIPLINE AND FRUSTRATION

There are many other foxes of frustration besides unpleasant aggravations, unfinished business, undue criticism, or unexpected delays. The best way to deal with life's little frustrations is to concentrate on the Christian life's little disciplines. When you neglect the simple, daily requirements of discipleship—praying and studying God's Word—you are a prime candidate to be ambushed by these little foxes.

> Be on your guard by building into your day the disciplines of prayer, solitude, and meditating on Scripture.

God is a God of detail. When you concentrate on doing the little things right, then frustrations have no power over you. Doctors Frank Minirth and Paul Meier note that the little things in our daily lives often determine how we feel.[37] From the time you get up in the morning to the time you go to bed, you face a number of scenarios and opportunities for the little foxes to attack your effectiveness. Be on your guard by building into your day the disciplines of prayer, solitude, and meditating on Scripture. As you struggle to deal with frustration, claim this encouraging word from the Lord, "There's more to come: We continue to shout our praise even when we're hemmed in with troubles, because we know how troubles can develop passionate patience in us, and how that patience in turn forges the tempered steel of virtue, keeping us alert for whatever God will do next." (Romans 5:3-4, The Message)

---

37 Frank B. Minirth and Paul B. Meier, *Happiness Is A Choice* (Grand Rapids, Michigan: Baker Book House, 1978), p. 176.

## TO THINK ABOUT:

- How do you typically express frustration?

- Why are "little foxes" the perfect description for frustration?

- How can clutter and disorganization reduce your effectiveness?

- What unfinished tasks are lurking on your to-do list? What action steps can you take to accomplish them?

- Think of a recent criticism you received. How can you find something positive in it?

- Why is *timing* more important than *time* from God's perspective?


## FOR THE FOLLOWING SCRIPTURES, ASK:

○ What does it say?    ○ What does it mean?    ○ How can you apply it?

- Romans 5:3-4
- James 1:19
- 2 Peter 3:8-9

# CHAPTER 10

# Uprooting Bitterness in Your Life

I once read a tragic story of jealous twin brothers whose father was a very wealthy businessman. The older brother was his father's favorite, but the younger son grew closer to his mother. The father had intended to give controlling interest in the family business to his oldest son, but his wife shrewdly helped the younger brother trick his own brother out of his legal rights.

When the father learned of this shady deal, he refused to recognize it. He remained determined to give his prosperous empire to his older son anyway. However, in the final act of his devious plan, the youngest son deceived his aging father and manipulated him into the legal transfer of the business to him. By the time the older brother learned of the unethical transaction, it was too late. He had lost everything. The older brother was enraged and publicly threatened to exact revenge by killing his brother (who quickly moved out of town, relocating the business with him). For many years, the older brother seethed with resentment and bitterness. He vowed that he would destroy his backstabbing brother if he ever saw his face again.

If you wonder if *People Magazine* reported that story, you are wrong. In fact, it is a story that comes from the Bible. It describes what happened 3,800 years ago between two brothers—Esau and

Jacob. When the writer of Hebrews addressed the problem of bitterness, he referred to this ancient feud:

> Make every effort to live in peace with all men and to be holy; without holiness no one will see the Lord. See to it that no one misses the grace of God and that no bitter root grows up to cause trouble and defile many. See that no one is sexually immoral, or is godless like Esau, who for a single meal sold his inheritance right as the oldest son. Afterward, as you know, when he wanted to inherit this blessing, he was rejected. He could bring about no change of mind, though he sought the blessing with tears. (Hebrews 12:14-17)

Bitterness is an insidious problem. It can initially reside undetected, or (if left untreated) it can overcome someone's entire personality. Are you currently harboring bitterness in your heart toward any person? Are you maintaining a grudge against anyone? In order to deal with a problem, you must first identify exactly what it is. Only then can you move on to overcoming its destructive effects.

........................................................

Bitterness is an insidious problem.
It can initially reside undetected, or
(if left untreated) it can overcome
someone's entire personality.

........................................................

## WHAT IS BITTERNESS?

Bitterness is an attitude of deep resentment and anger that refuses to be reconciled. The word *bitter* describes something with a bad taste. When I was in high school, one of my classmates handed me a green persimmon and invited me to take a bite. He assured me that it tasted sweet. I hope that you have never bitten into a green persimmon. I can personally testify that it makes your mouth pucker up so that all you can do is whistle! When I think of bitterness, I think of the unpalatable taste of that green persimmon.

Bitterness not only describes a bad taste in your mouth but also a bad attitude in your heart. The English word *bitter* is from the Anglo-Saxon word *biter*, meaning "piercingly harsh, cruel, caustic, or acrimonious." We have all known someone who possessed a sarcastic, sardonic attitude. Nobody enjoys being around someone like that. The word used in the New Testament for bitterness is the Greek word *pikros*, which means, "to cut or to prick." We are tempted to become bitter after someone hurts us.

········································································

# We don't always realize when bitterness has taken hold in our lives.

········································································

We don't always realize when bitterness has taken hold in our lives. Why is that? It can cause an emotional "blind spot." We think we are doing a good job of hiding our hurt, but carrying bitterness in our heart can severely damage our spirit, like a caustic acid that destroys its own container. When resentment builds in your heart, it will slowly damage your personality.

In 1977, I served as pastor in a church in central Alabama. I had recently graduated from Southern Seminary in Louisville, Kentucky, and approached my new job with a great spirit of zeal and optimism about the Lord's work. Several longtime pastors in the area invited some of the younger preachers in the area to meet each Friday to fellowship, pray, and then have lunch. I will never forget one of the older pastors shaking his head after I had just finished sharing about the exciting events that were happening in our little church. He said, "There was a time I used to be idealistic like you. However, through the years I have become cynical, hardened, and skeptical because I have found that the meanest people you will ever encounter are in church."

My naïve, immediate response was, "Surely, there aren't mean people in the church!" (I have since discovered that there was a measure of truth in his cynical statement.) I remember asking God to keep me from being like this pastor, whose ministry was marked by mediocrity. The resentment and pain he carried was causing him great agony, and misery had etched deep lines of concern on his face. Bitterness causes much more damage to the person who is carrying it than to the ones who may have caused it.

## BITTERNESS BEGINS SMALL

Not only does bitterness hurt the person who carries it inside, but it also poisons others. Hebrews 12:15 says, "See to it that no one misses the grace of God and that no bitter root grows up to cause trouble and defile many." I like the imagery of a tiny root because bitterness may begin small like a tiny sliver of a root. Maybe you nurse an emotional wound you received from a friend or colleague just a little too long. Then you start remembering every time this person hurt you in the past. Soon, you find yourself dwelling on and reliving similar hurtful experiences you've had with others. Your temper gets shorter. You become suspicious of those who might hurt you. Your relationships become strained. Bitterness can start small, but it can grow and damage many people.

· · · · · · · · · · · · · · · · · · · · · · · · · · · · · · · · · · · · · · · · · · · · · ·

## Not only does bitterness hurt the person who carries it inside, but it also poisons others.

· · · · · · · · · · · · · · · · · · · · · · · · · · · · · · · · · · · · · · · · · · · · · ·

Workplace violence is on the rise in America today where disgruntled employees take vengeance on their bosses or coworkers. Hopefully, your bitterness toward someone at work will never lead to such tragic actions. However, the probability is great that your personal resentment will hurt those around you in some way. You may lash out emotionally rather than physically, but holding a grudge always causes pain.

What causes a resentful spirit? Bitterness can be directed toward various targets, for many reasons. It is possible for you to be bitter toward God. Perhaps you prayed for God to do something in the past and you felt that He did not answer your prayer. Maybe you asked Him to heal a family member, restore a marriage, or help you out during a tough time. I have also encountered many people who are bitter toward the church. "I'll never darken the doors of that church again," people will say to me on occasion. Why? Somewhere in the past, a church did something that they disagreed with, or someone in the church said or did something to offend them. Such people often receive a bizarre sense of satisfaction in nursing grudges, and they miss out on finding true fellowship among Christians in a loving church. Not only that, they let their grudge keep them from growing in their relationship with God.

## Bitterness can be growing just below the surface, its presence undetected.

While some people make it obvious that they are consumed by resentment, most of us are unaware at the beginning stages of bitterness in our hearts. We start internalizing our hurts and making a mental list of people who have hurt our feelings at work, at church, or in our circle of friends. Before we know it, our list has become quite long! Before you insist that you don't need to finish this chapter on bitterness because it doesn't apply to you, think again. Identifying bitterness in your life is often difficult because the biblical imagery of a root is underground, invisible to our eyes. Likewise, bitterness can be growing just below the surface, its presence undetected.

Several years ago, I tackled the job of cleaning some jasmine vines out of our flowerbed. Thinking I would save some time, I made the mistake of cutting off the vines at ground level. For several days, everything looked fine. However, when I chopped off the vines without removing the root, it was like pruning the plants to make them stronger. The vines returned with a vengeance. This time, I spent several hours digging in the dirt to remove the roots. I was surprised to see how big the roots were and how widely distributed they were underneath the ground. It was hard, backbreaking work, but I finally extracted most of the roots and the vines did not grow back.

··················································································

## You can detect a root of bitterness by recognizing the bad fruit that it produces.

··················································································

Ask yourself the following questions. Any "yes" answer reveals that you may possess bitterness and need to seek peace with someone.

1.  Is there anyone against whom you hold a grudge?
2.  Is there anyone you haven't forgiven?
3.  Are there any misunderstandings you are unwilling to forget?
4.  Is there any person against whom you are harboring bitterness or resentment?
5.  Are you quick to find fault?
6.  Are you carrying hidden anger?
7.  Do you ever by word or deed seek to hurt someone?
8.  Do you gossip?
9.  Do you speak unkindly about people when they are not present?
10. Is there anyone with whom you are unwilling to be reconciled?

Have you made the mistake of simply trying to deal with the results or "fruit" of your bitterness, rather than getting to the root of the problem? Have you told yourself that you'll just try harder to control your temper or be nicer to people? You can detect a root of bitterness by recognizing the bad fruit that it produces. However, the only way to deal with the problem is to attack the root, rather than simply try to destroy the fruit.

## ROOTS AND FRUITS OF BITTERNESS

Sometimes we have a hard time seeing the relationship between the various roots of bitterness and their corresponding fruits. When we can trace our actions and attitudes back to their source, we begin to understand how we can deal with the problem.

### Anger Leads to Hatred

Hatred is anger in full bloom. However, hatred is hard to identify. If I asked if you hated anyone, you would likely reply, "Of course not." However, hatred is borne from any desire to harm someone. If you carry a desire to hurt someone or to see that person suffer harm in any way, it is evidence of the root of anger. Someone may be able to repress the bitter root of seething anger for a time, but it will often show its fruit in a sudden, violent fit. If you don't deal with it immediately, the root may spread insidiously, producing its fruit in mental or physical illness.

......................................................................................

If you don't deal with it immediately, the root may spread insidiously, producing its fruit in mental or physical illness.

......................................................................................

Aesop's Fables tell the story of a man who hated his neighbors. In this fable, he met with Zeus, who said, "I will grant you any wish that you want. The only stipulation is that I will grant to your neighbors, whom you hate, twice as much of whatever you ask. If you ask for 500 diamonds, your neighbor will receive 1,000."

The man agonized over the wish he should request of Zeus. So intense was his hatred for his neighbor that finally he said, "I wish you to make me blind in one eye."

························································

## Resentment is also a hard-to-detect attitude because we can bury our hurt underground, like a root.

························································

This is the malicious attitude of some people who have grown irrational with bitterness. They hope to inflict pain on others, even if and when it results in their own pain. Remember, bitterness is an acid that destroys its own container. You may relish in the idea that you are hurting someone by focusing on how much you hate that person, but you are hurting yourself much more.

### Resentment Leads to Revenge

Resentment is also a hard-to-detect attitude because we can bury our hurt underground, like a root. However, the corresponding fruit soon becomes obvious; it is the desire for revenge. You may resent someone's offensive attitudes or actions. You've heard it said, "I don't get mad, I get even." People often say vengeance is sweet, but it is not. It is sour. Being stung by a wasp and then killing the wasp doesn't take away the pain of its sting. Resentment is the root of bitterness that produces the bad fruit of revenge. The only people with whom you should try to get even are those who have helped you.

### Grudges Lead to Meanness

Grudges have long roots. Nursing a grudge is the long-term action we take after we are offended. We tighten our grip on our pain instead of letting it go. The fruit of holding a grudge is meanness. Examine your relationships. Have you been mean to those around you? Maybe you say something in jest, but it comes across in a mean way. Our culture has developed a word for people who are mean—"haters." Some people enjoy being mean to others. There is even a saying among some unscrupulous attorneys that if the facts are on your side, argue the facts; if the law is on your side, argue the law; but if neither the facts nor the law are on your side, attack the witness. The end never does justify the meanness!

························································································

# The only people with whom you should try to get even are those who have helped you.

························································································

### *Animosity Leads to Rejection*

Bitterness can also be expressed as animosity. Animosity is a strong dislike of another person. It has not evolved into full-throttle hatred, but it may go back to some unpleasant childhood experience or damage from a dysfunctional family relationship. You may express animosity toward men or toward women in general today because you have gone through a messy divorce and you have not forgiven your ex-spouse. Animosity is often expressed by marking a person off of your list of friends. You may have animosity toward an entire family. You don't want your kids to be friends with their kids. You don't want your friends or family to be nice to that family. You know you have allowed the root of animosity to grow in your heart if you refuse to have anything to do with certain people anymore.

## BREAKING THE CYCLE OF BITTERNESS

Bitterness produces an unpleasant hostility cycle of retaliation that feeds on itself as it grows. It says, "Because you have hurt me in a minor way, I'll retaliate by doing something worse to you. If you hurt me in a major way, you can be assured I'll give you more of the same."

When I first published this book in 1993, the latest research was that there were over 100,000 teenage gang members in America—and that was alarming. Today, according to the FBI, there are over 33,000 individual gangs and about 1.4 million criminally active members.[38] The "gang mindset" is always concerned with payback. What are you supposed to do when someone slaps your face? Jesus told us, "If someone strikes you on the right cheek, turn to him the other also." (Matthew 5:39) While many of us are not being slapped physically, we may endure plenty of emotional slaps. The only thing that will break the hostility cycle is one person's willingness to absorb an injustice without retaliation. This was the attitude of the Lord Jesus Christ. In 1 Peter 2:23, we read, "When they hurled their insults at him, he did not retaliate; when he suffered, he made no threats. Instead, he entrusted himself to him who judges justly."

· · · · · · · · · · · · · · · · · · · · · · · · · · · · · · · · · · · · · · · · · · · · · · ·

## While many of us are not being slapped physically, we may endure plenty of emotional slaps.

· · · · · · · · · · · · · · · · · · · · · · · · · · · · · · · · · · · · · · · · · · · · · · ·

Open your heart to God and ask Him to inspect it for any trace of meanness, a desire to hurt others, or a desire to get even. The Bible gives us the words to pray:

> Investigate my life, O God, find out everything about me; Cross-examine and test me, get a clear picture of what I'm about; See for yourself whether I've done anything wrong—then guide me on the road to eternal life. (Psalm 139:23-24, The Message)

Recognize the fruit of bitterness. Then attack the root. Attack it by confessing it to the Lord and asking His forgiveness.

---

38  FBI website, http://www.fbi.gov/about-us/investigate/vc_majorthefts/gangs, accessed September 1, 2014.

### Seek to Reconcile

What will grow in place of bitterness? Hebrews 12:14 gives us the positive replacement for the root of bitterness: "Make every effort to live in peace with all men and to be holy." When we honor our responsibility to be right with others, we are right with God.

What does it mean to seek peace with other people? The language in Hebrews 12 suggests that we are to run after peace, to pursue it as a worthy goal. However, it is not possible to live at peace with everyone in the world because some people simply won't allow it. That's why Paul tells us, "If it is possible, *as far as it depends on you, live at peace with everyone.*" (Romans 12:18, emphasis added) Peace at any price is too high a price to pay. We can never compromise our conviction simply for the sake of peace. We can't force someone to reconcile. However, we must strive to live at peace; that should be our goal.

## When we honor our responsibility to be right with others, we are right with God.

When there is peace in your heart, there will be corresponding fruit produced in your life. Instead of anger, there will be an attitude of reconciliation. As you take the first step to initiate peace with someone, you obey God. No matter how the person responds—favorably or otherwise—you can know you have done the right thing by trying to reconcile your relationship.

One of my favorite books is *How Green Was My Valley* by Richard Llewellyn. In this moving story about a Welsh mining family, a young boy falls into icy water and is temporarily paralyzed. The young man, who had been so full of energy and life, transforms into a morose and bitter person. He is ready to give up on life. However, his pastor, friends, and family won't allow that. One day they carry

him to the top of a mountain. There, overlooking his little village, he
experiences a wonderful freedom from his resentment.

Llewellyn writes:

> I went out, and up on top of the mountain to have peace,
> for I had a grudge that was savaged with heat against
> everybody and only up on top there where it was green and
> high and blue and quiet, with only the winds to come at
> you was a place of rest—there the unkindness of man for
> man could be forgotten and I could wait for God to send
> calm and wisdom.[39]

Let's walk through the garden of your life and replace the
"bitter roots" with some pleasant character traits. Instead of the
bitter root of hatred, you should plant love, the first fruit of the
Spirit mentioned in Galatians 5:22. Have you ever noticed that
bitterness always keeps a tally of past hurts? Love is just the opposite.
According to 1 Corinthians 13:5, love "keeps no record of wrong."

........................................................................

# They do not deserve your forgiveness any more than you deserve for God to forgive you.

........................................................................

Instead of the root of resentment and the fruit of revenge,
forgiveness should blossom in your life. You must be willing
to forgive those who have committed an injustice against you.
Although they mistreated you, gossiped about you, and hurt you,
forgive them. They do not deserve your forgiveness any more
than you deserve for God to forgive you. Jesus makes it clear that
we are to forgive those who sin against us. He taught the disciples
to pray, "Forgive us our debts, as we also have forgiven our

---

39   Richard Llewellyn, *How Green Was My Valley* (New York: McMillan Company, 1940), p. 451.

debtors." (Matthew 6:12) Forgiveness does not make what they did to you okay—it makes *you* okay (spiritually and emotionally whole again).

····································································

# Try showing kindness to those around you and see if you don't receive kindness in return.

····································································

Simon Peter once asked the Lord if he had to forgive someone as many as seven times, and Jesus surprised him with His reply. He said, "I tell you, not seven times, but seventy-seven times." (Matthew 18:22) In other words, there is no limit to the number of times that we should be willing to forgive. Forgiveness is the key that unlocks your chains of resentment, destroys the root of bitterness, and sets you free.

Instead of holding a grudge, try the tender fruit of kindness. Practice the advice found in Ephesians 4:32: "Be kind and compassionate to one another, forgiving each other, just as in Christ God forgave you." If you were paid one dollar for every kind word you spoke last year, but you had to pay 25 cents for every unkind word you spoke, what would be your balance? Kindness is love with its work clothes on. Try showing kindness to those around you and see if you don't receive kindness in return.

Instead of letting animosity lead to the rejection of others, we should also practice being more accepting of all Christians. Jesus is the head of the Body of Christ, the Church. The Church is a beautiful blending of the full variety of individuals and their gifts. Paul makes a comparison to the human body in 1 Corinthians 12:12-30. Just as in your physical body, every part is important. We tend to think that some parts of the body are not very important. For instance, we may wonder about the value of our little toe. Some say God gave us a little toe so that we could find the bedpost in the middle of the night when the light is out! In the same way, there may be some people in the Body of Christ that you think are not important. However, when one member hurts, all of the Body hurts. We should strive to accept everyone who is a child of God as part of our family.

········································································

# Let's be sure that as Christians we help the weak and accept the hurting.

········································································

The church is an organism rather than an organization. Do you know the difference? When there is a weak part in an organization, it is cut out. That's why businesses often restructure and eliminate many jobs. However, in an organism like the human body, the rest of the body goes to the aid of any weak part to provide assistance. Let's be sure that as Christians we help the weak and accept the hurting.

## CURING BITTERNESS

Do you remember the two brothers at the beginning of the chapter? The rest of the story is in Genesis 31 and 32. After a number of years living on the run, the younger brother Jacob decided he wanted to be closer to his homeland. However, how would his older brother Esau react? He received word from messengers that Esau had assembled an army of 400 men to meet him. Jacob was terrified. He divided his family into separate groups so if Esau attacked one group, the others could escape. Before the inevitable confrontation, Jacob agonized in prayer all night. In an amazing encounter with God, the Bible says he wrestled with an angel. Jacob finally got right with God and vowed that he wouldn't release the angel until God blessed him.

Jacob changed that day to become a true worshiper. God even changed his name from Jacob to Israel.

....................................................................

## Ask God for His help as you seek to replace bitterness with peace.

....................................................................

The next morning, this changed man went out to confront his brother. Israel was no longer a liar, a cheat, and a schemer like the old Jacob. God had transformed Israel from within and replaced his treachery and selfishness with love and a desire for peace. He approached his brother and bowed down before him, awaiting his vengeance. Instead of killing him as he had promised, Esau ran to his brother, and they embraced in a tearful reunion. For most of their adult lives, bitterness and resentment had surrounded their relationship. Finally, there was peace and reconciliation. How many years have you wasted because of bitterness? The good news is that it's never too late to change. Ask God for His help as you seek to replace bitterness with peace.

## TO THINK ABOUT:

- How would you define a bitter spirit in your own words?

- What is it like to be around someone with a bitter attitude?

- How can bitterness and resentment begin small and grow?

- How is it possible to be unaware of resentment building in your heart?

- What is the difference between dealing with bitterness at the root or fruit level?

- In what way is a bitter, sarcastic attitude contagious? At home? At work? Among friends?

- You break the cycle of hostility when you are "willing to absorb an injustice without retaliation." How does that work? Have you ever experienced that? Explain.

## FOR THE FOLLOWING SCRIPTURES, ASK:
○ What does it say?    ○ What does it mean?    ○ How can you apply it?

- 1 Corinthians 13:4-8
- Ephesians 4:29
- Philippians 2:14-16

# CHAPTER 11

# Anger: Reaching the Boiling Point

S everal years ago, my wife and I were driving through downtown Birmingham, Alabama. At an intersection, a car pulled out into the lane in front of the car ahead of us, which caused it to brake suddenly. I watched with amusement and then with alarm as the man who'd had to apply his brakes blew his horn and proceeded to tailgate the car that had pulled in front of him. When we stopped at the next traffic light, the angry man jumped out, ran up to the car in front of him and started pounding on the roof of the car, shouting obscenities. He was red in the face as he invited the driver of the car to step out and fight. Fortunately, the other driver did not accept his invitation. Scenes like the exchange of road rage that took place that day on the streets of Birmingham occur every day across America and often fill the nightly news. Sometimes, road rage even ends in tragedy.

We live in the age of an overabundance of anger. We've had to invent terms like "road rage" to describe our violent tendencies. Researchers have now coined the phrase "customer rage" to describe dissatisfied customers who yell and curse at customer service personnel on the phone and in person. The threads in the online comments sections of a news article or a product review often devolve into a verbal brawl between two or three people who trade insults for expressing a different opinion. We are an angry society, and we're willing to take it out on anyone at anytime.

Amidst all our growing discontent, some people have just simply learned to put up with anger as part of modern living. However, having an even disposition does not mean being angry all the time. Can a Christian be angry? Does all anger constitute sin? What are the limits of our anger? If you have a problem with anger or live with people who mismanage their anger, you need to understand the biblical teaching about it. The Bible is full of teachings about dealing with anger. Consider these passages from Proverbs.

> A short-tempered man is a fool. He hates the man who is patient. (Proverbs 14:17, TLB)

> A wise man controls his temper. He knows that anger causes mistakes. (Proverbs 14:29, TLB)

> A hot-tempered man must pay the penalty; if you rescue him, you will have to do it again. (Proverbs 19:19)

· · · · · · · · · · · · · · · · · · · · · · · · · · · · · · · · · · · · · · · · · · · · · · · · · ·

## Can a Christian be angry? Does all anger constitute sin? What are the limits of our anger?

· · · · · · · · · · · · · · · · · · · · · · · · · · · · · · · · · · · · · · · · · · · · · · · · · ·

I like what Paul wrote about anger in Ephesians 4:26, 31-32:

> In your anger do not sin. Do not let the sun go down while you are still angry . . . Get rid of all bitterness, rage and anger, brawling and slander, along with every form of malice. Be kind and compassionate to one another, forgiving each other, just as in Christ God forgave you.

In this passage, Paul uses three different words to describe different kinds of anger. The Greek language is more precise than English, and it allows for more meaningful descriptions of the same word. First, Paul mentions "rage" in the list of things we are to get rid of. However, there is another kind of sinful anger besides this harsh, raging anger. In verse 26, he says not to let the sun set "while you are still angry." The word he uses here for "angry" means a type of hidden anger. However, Paul describes another kind of anger in verse 26 when he writes: "In your anger do not sin." This is a different word than rage or hidden anger. The word refers to holy anger or righteous indignation. It's possible to be angry and not sin. Understanding and distinguishing between sinful anger and appropriate anger is necessary in dealing with this problem.

...........................................................

There is a harmful kind of anger that spreads like wildfire consuming everything in its path.

...........................................................

## RAGING ANGER

In Ephesians 4:31, Paul uses the word *thumos*. This word is translated "rage" in the New International Version. It describes a blazing fire. There is a harmful kind of anger that spreads like wildfire consuming everything in its path. This is explosive, harsh, uncontrolled anger. We have many phrases to describe this kind of violent anger. Do you recognize any of these?

> *"I just blew my stack!"*
> *"I lost my cool!"*
> *"That just makes my blood boil!"*
> *"I'm ticked off!"*
> *"It just makes me see red!"*

We usually describe this kind of anger as "losing one's temper." Psychologists have even coined a term for a person who has little control over his temper—rageaholic. You may be a rageaholic; or worse, you may have to live with a rageaholic. Maybe you work for a rageaholic. This kind of destructive anger always hurts people. Will Rogers once quipped, "When a person flies off into a rage, he seldom makes a good landing."

......................................................................................
## Psychologists have even coined a term for a person who has little control over his temper—rageaholic.
......................................................................................

The Bible recognizes this kind of anger as sin that should be avoided. Ephesians 4:31 admonishes us to "get rid" of it. When you lose your temper, you risk losing so much more than just your self-control.

For example, when you lose your temper, you can sometimes lose your job. A rageaholic poisons a work atmosphere for those around him. When I was a teenager, I watched Ohio State University play in the Gator Bowl. The legendary coach, Woody Hayes, led Ohio State to many victories. During this particular game, an opposing player intercepted one of Ohio State's passes at a critical time in the game. As the offense tackled the opposing player near the Ohio State sideline, Coach Hayes became so incensed that he momentarily lost control. In front of a national television audience, he grabbed the opposing player and began to pound him with his fist. His assistant coaches had to pull him off the player. As a result of that highly publicized incident, a great football coach lost his job and his reputation, all because he lost his temper.

When you continually lose your temper, you may also lose your marriage. There are some "closet rageaholics" who only lose their temper at home with their family. They would never do so at church or on the job. I've seen many marriages damaged by a spouse—husbands *and* wives—who continually displayed this kind of harmful anger.

When you lose your temper, you may also lose your friends. Few people enjoy being around someone who is angry all the time. I enjoy playing golf with other men. However, no one enjoys playing with a golfer who curses and throws his clubs whenever he makes a bad shot. He spoils the round for everyone else.

A golfing buddy of mine once read about a man who got so mad after a particularly poor shot that he turned and threw his club toward his golf cart. According to this account, the club hit on the bar supporting the roof of the cart, and the head of the club broke off from the shaft. The broken shaft boomeranged back toward the golfer, and the jagged end penetrated the man's neck, cutting his coronary artery. He died before he could get medical attention. This is an extreme example, but when he lost his temper, he lost his life!

· · · · · · · · · · · · · · · · · · · · · · · · · · · · · · · · · · · · · · · · · · · · · · · · · · · · · ·

## When you lose your temper, you risk losing so much more than just your self-control.

· · · · · · · · · · · · · · · · · · · · · · · · · · · · · · · · · · · · · · · · · · · · · · · · · · · · · ·

When you lose your temper, you may also lose your health. Dr. Walker Cannon, a professor at Harvard University, describes what happens to a person when he is angry:

> Respiration deepens; the heart beats more rapidly; the arterial pressure rises; the blood is shifted from the stomach and intestines to the heart, central nervous system, and the muscles; the process of the alimentary canal ceases; sugar is freed from the reserves in the liver; the spleen contracts and discharges its contents of concentrated corpuscles, and adrenaline is secreted.[40]

If you think you can blow up at someone and return to normal—think again. Isolated incidents of rage may not harm us, but continual

---

40  Paul Lee Tan, *Signs Of The Times* (Rockville, Maryland: Assurance Publishers, 1979), p. 30.

and frequent outbursts of anger will damage our health. It would be helpful if humans came with a warning sticker: "Caution! The Word of God has determined that losing your temper can be harmful to your life."

........................................................

# If you think you can blow up at someone and return to normal— think again.

........................................................

The important question is, "What does it take to make you extremely angry?" The size of a person's character can generally be determined by the size of whatever makes him lose his temper. Some people lose their temper about seemingly insignificant things. An old proverb says, "The emptier the pot, the quicker it boils." What is your personal boiling point?

## HIDDEN ANGER

There is another kind of sinful anger besides harsh, raging anger. In Ephesians 4:26, the Bible says, "Do not let the sun go down when you are still angry." While *thumos* is rage expressed, the word Paul uses for this kind of anger, *perorgismo*, is rage repressed. It is hidden anger. The only difference between these two kinds of anger is that one is below the surface while the other has already erupted. *Thumos* is anger that explodes like a volcano, whereas *perorgismo* is anger that simmers, stews, and smolders. When sufficiently agitated, it usually develops into *thumos*.

Hidden anger is unresolved anger. Retaining hidden anger over a long period can be very dangerous. It can be compared to filling a metal trashcan with paper, setting it on fire and then shutting it in a closet in your home. The fire may burn itself out, but it will probably burn down your home! If you do not deal with your unresolved anger, you are likely to suffer as a result.

### Angry with God

Hidden anger is much like its first cousin, bitterness, because they both exist just below the surface. Also like bitterness, we sometimes direct our hidden anger toward God. People who tend to repress their anger toward God feel that He has shortchanged them in life. Or perhaps they feel that God did not respond to their desperate prayers. Or they may be silently angry because others seem to be prospering more than they are at work, at home, or in life in general. People who are angry with God seldom express their anger by shaking their fists toward heaven and screaming. Instead, they keep it inside, but they are not letting God off the hook.

### Angry with Yourself

I often say that the person in our church with whom I have the most trouble is my wife's first husband—me. When I was younger, I was very self-critical and prone to condemn myself. When you are angry with yourself, that anger is nonproductive. Self-directed anger prevents us from enjoying our identity in Christ. If you are too hard on yourself, try to loosen up and allow yourself greater latitude to make mistakes. Nobody is perfect except Jesus Christ.

> People who tend to repress their anger toward God feel that He has shortchanged them in life.

### Angry with Authority

Some people harbor anger toward those in authority over them. Many teenagers stay angry with their parents and resent their authority. They simply keep it bottled up within. Others are angry toward their bosses at work and fantasize about the day they "tell their bosses off" and quit their jobs. When we carry this kind of hidden anger toward other people in authority, we actually are hurting ourselves. In his book, *None Of These Diseases*, Dr. S. I. McMillan writes about the consequences of carrying hidden anger toward another person:

> The moment I start hating a man, I become his slave. I can't even enjoy my work anymore because he even controls my thoughts. My resentment produces too many stress hormones in my body and I become fatigued after only a few hours of work. The man I hate hounds me wherever I go. I cannot escape his tyrannical grasp on my mind. When the waiter serves me Porterhouse steak with French fries, crisp salad, and strawberry shortcake smothered with ice cream, it might as well be stale bread and water. My teeth chew the food and I swallow it, but the man I hate won't let me enjoy it. The man I hate may be miles from my bedroom, but more cruel than any slave driver. He whips my thoughts into such a frenzy that even my innerspring mattress becomes a rack of torture.[41]

What is the danger of allowing hidden anger to accumulate day after day? Paul writes in Ephesians 4:27 not to "give the devil a foothold." Your evil adversary is always looking for little cracks in your personality. Unresolved anger is a crack into which he can easily slip a wedge of temptation to cause division and pain.

............................................................

# Unresolved anger is a crack into which he can easily slip a wedge of temptation to cause division and pain.

............................................................

One of the places where unresolved anger does its worst damage is in a marriage. Imagine a husband and a wife whose animated

---

41  S. I. McMillan, M.D., *None Of These Diseases* (Old Tappan: Spire Books, 1986), p. 72.

disagreement turns into a full-blown argument. The argument progresses until a great deal of anger crackles in the air, and the exchange borders on fighting. After a night of arguing without resolution, they simply go to bed, turn their backs to each other, and allow their anger to simmer and seethe. What they are actually doing is inviting the devil to come into their marriage and destroy it. Satan will use unresolved anger to divide their union. Unresolved anger in a marriage is like an untreated flesh wound. If it is not dealt with, emotional infection can set in and the damage may be irreparable.

·············································································

## When we carry this kind of hidden anger toward other people in authority, we actually are hurting ourselves.

·············································································

The devil notices when little sparks of anger fly between husbands and wives, family members, and friends. He then fans the unresolved anger into roaring flames before sitting down in front of the fire, where he warms himself and laughs at our misery.

## PRACTICAL WAYS TO ADDRESS ANGER

The Bible identifies rage and hidden anger as equally sinful. The following are some practical suggestions for how to conquer both types.

### Try to Control Your Anger

First of all, make an intentional attempt to control your temper. Some may say, "Wait a minute! That's just my problem; I can't control my temper!" However, think about what you are saying. Since we have available to us the power of God, when we don't control our temper, we're saying in effect, "I *won't* allow God to control my temper."

The Bible says, "Those who control their anger have great understanding; those with a hasty temper will make mistakes." (Proverbs 14:29, NLT) If you still insist that you can't take control of your anger, see if you can relate to these two scenes. John and Mary have been married for 20 years. They have a rocky relationship because they often argue, and John tends to lose his temper and start screaming. Mary's defense mechanism is simply to shut herself into her room and cry. She doesn't want to deal with the issue. One day John and Mary get into one of their heated arguments, and John is hollering at his wife. He has obviously lost his temper. Suddenly the telephone rings. Mary answers it and tells John that it is his boss. John takes the phone and in a calm, collected voice says, "Hi, Jim. How can I help you?" Only moments before, John seemed totally out of control. But when he learned his boss was on the phone, he instantly had the ability to control his anger. He was still mad, but his temper was under control. Can you relate to this kind of experience?

......................................................................

## Maturity involves choosing the correct emotional response, even if it contradicts our negative feelings.

......................................................................

Consider another scenario. Mike and Kay have been married for five years and have two active preschoolers. It takes an act of Congress to get everyone up, dressed, and fed on Sunday mornings. It is often a frustrating, harrowing experience. As they are driving to church, Kay begins to nag Mike because he doesn't give her more help with the children. Mike retaliates by naming all the pressure he is under at work. By the time they arrive at church, both kids are crying and Mike and Kay are red in the face from screaming. When they pull into the church parking lot and get out of their car, one of their friends from Sunday school greets them. Mike and Kay quickly put on their best smiles and say something like, "Praise the Lord! Isn't this a beautiful day to worship Jesus?"

## The first step in addressing anger is calling on your own self-discipline not to lose your temper.

We possess the willpower to change from anger to cheerfulness whenever we so desire. We can choose to refrain from sinful anger. Maturity involves choosing the correct emotional response, even if it contradicts our negative feelings. If you suspect that you are a rageaholic, ask those closest to you; they will be happy to tell you! Like an alcoholic, your first step to recovery from rageaholism is to admit that you have a problem. If you are living with a rageaholic, you may need to lovingly intervene. Let the person know that you are struggling to cope with his rage. Tell him that he is making your life and your family miserable. There is help available, but recognizing the problem is a prerequisite.

### Admit You Cannot Solve Your Problem Alone

The first step in addressing anger is calling on your own self-discipline not to lose your temper. We know this is possible because we use willpower all the time to our own benefit. However, the second step toward recovery is counterintuitive to the first one. You must admit that you cannot solve your problem on your own. So, which is it? Self-control or surrender? The answer is, "Yes." It's both.

You must practice self-control, while depending on another power—that is, the power of Jesus Christ to give you strength to overcome your anger for good. As you work on controlling your temper, you may need to pray 12-15 times a day, asking God to keep your anger in check. You can be honest with Him. Simply pray, "God, I have a problem with anger. You know that I am so mad at this person that I am ready to lose it. Help me control my temper at this time." Whenever you stop praying for God to give you strength, your temper can get out of control again despite your best efforts.

### Mind What You Say

Another suggestion for dealing with sinful anger is to guard your tongue carefully. We most often express anger by what we say. Some people slam their foot on the accelerator when they get angry. Others slam the door and walk out. However, we most often cause damage when we open our mouths. In Romans 12:1 Paul writes, "Therefore, I urge you brothers, in view of God's mercy, to offer your bodies as living sacrifices, holy and pleasing to God—this is your spiritual act of worship." Christians offer their bodies—including their mouths—as living sacrifices for God's use. Ask God to shut your mouth before you speak words of anger. Those who stubbornly refuse to speak to the object of their anger for the rest of the day may twist this principle into justifying their behavior. Remember, unresolved anger is just as sinful as anger expressed.

......................................................

## Another suggestion for dealing with sinful anger is to guard your tongue carefully.

......................................................

A Christian who expresses sinful verbal anger is a living contradiction. James writes, "With the tongue we praise our Lord and Father, and with it we curse men, who have been made in God's likeness. Out of the same mouth come praise and cursing. My brothers, this should not be." (James 3:9-10)

When I was in college, I taped a card with a memory verse to the mirror in my dormitory room. It was Proverbs 15:1, which says, "A gentle answer turns away wrath, but a harsh word stirs up anger." When someone directs anger toward you, one of the best ways to repel it is to respond softly and gently. On the other hand, if you retaliate with more anger, it only exacerbates the problem. Be careful what you say when you are angry. You may have heard the expression, "When you get angry, count to 10 before you speak." I have better advice. When you get angry, count to 100 and then don't say anything!

### Watch Your Witness

Another way to deal with sinful anger is to consider your Christian testimony. Christians who lose their temper have helped turn many non-Christians away from the faith. I can honestly say that the Lord has helped me become a man who is not easily upset by much of anything. However, there was a time when I struggled to control my anger.

.........................................................................................

## Christians who lose their temper have helped turn many non-Christians away from the faith.

.........................................................................................

When I was playing sports in high school, I was extremely competitive. I recall a certain basketball game during my senior year when an official made what I believed to be poor calls. I had driven to the basket and been hacked a few times by my opponents, but the referee had not called a foul. Each time I ran back up the court, I would inform him of his oversight. I think I also questioned the quality of his vision. After a few minutes, the referee blew his whistle, pointed at me, and shouted, "Number 34, you are out of the game!" I remember the entire gymnasium grew quiet. In front of my parents and the entire student body, I had to walk off the court because I had lost my temper.

As I sat on the bench, I began to regret my outburst. I was recognized as a committed Christian. I stood up for Christ, witnessed to my friends, and even led a campus Bible study. I realized that I had hurt my testimony. I resolved from that point on to do a better job of guarding my temper.

If you are a believer, will you allow God to speak to your heart and influence you to avoid sinful anger? It will save you from a lifetime of heartache. God wants you to respond with grace and love so that others will recognize there is a difference in your life because of Jesus Christ.

## RIGHTEOUS ANGER

You may be surprised to learn that not all anger is sinful. There is another kind of anger mentioned in the Bible. In Ephesians 4:26 Paul says, "In your anger do not sin." This is an entirely different word than *thumos* and *perorgismo*. The word here is *orge*. This is holy anger or righteous indignation. It sounds like a contradiction in terms, doesn't it?

This statement is made in the imperative mode in Greek, which means it is actually a command.

.......................................................................

# Christians are commanded to be angry about the things that make God angry.

.......................................................................

Christians are commanded to be angry about the things that make God angry. Jesus manifested this kind of righteous indignation when He got in trouble with the Pharisees for healing a man on the Sabbath. In response to their religiosity and hypocrisy, Jesus became angry because they were more concerned about rituals and rules than they were the needs of people. "Jesus looked around at them in anger and, deeply distressed at their stubborn hearts, said to the man, 'Stretch out your hand.' He stretched it out, and his hand was completely restored." (Mark 3:5) Just as Jesus expressed this kind of righteous indignation, we should be "good and angry" at certain times.

···········································································

## Just as Jesus expressed this kind of righteous indignation, we should be "good and angry" at certain times.

···········································································

There are many causes about which Christians should be angry. I am angry about the killing of unborn babies in America. From 1973-2011, nearly 53 million legal abortions have occurred in America.[42] There are laws to protect the unborn of animals. It is a federal crime to steal or otherwise hurt the egg of a bald or golden eagle. How ironic that so few people are protecting unborn human babies. I'm not angry toward any physician or clinic or person who performs abortions. I'm not upset at someone who chooses to have an abortion. However, I am outraged at the act and injustice of abortion, and I am praying and working to do everything within the law to see that these injustices change. That's righteous indignation.

## GOOD AND ANGRY

Righteous indignation is always directed toward an injustice, crime, or sin, not toward a person. One of the best tests to determine the validity of your anger is to ask, "Am I angry with a person, or do I have a settled kind of anger against that person's behavior?" Christians should be angry about legalized abortion in our country and a host of other issues in our culture today, including the degrading impact of pornography. I have witnessed how pornography has destroyed marriages and chained men and women in total bondage to its sinister addiction. Pornography makes victims

---

42   According to the latest available records from the Guttmacher Institute, http://www. guttmacher.org/pubs/fb_induced_abortion.html, accessed September 1, 2014.

of men, women, and children as well. I am directing my anger toward this injustice, not toward any person. Be careful to ensure that your anger is righteous indignation against sin, not vengeance against the sinner. The only kind of anger that is acceptable to God is the kind that is not directed toward hurting another person.

## BEING VICTORIOUS OVER ANGER

Dwight D. Eisenhower was recognized as a strong leader during World War II as he led our Allied Forces and later when he was elected President of our country. When Eisenhower was a child, he had a violent temper. One Halloween, he was not allowed to go trick-or-treating with his older brothers. He was so enraged by his parents' decision that he ran out of the house to an apple tree in his yard and began pounding his fist into its trunk until his fists bled. His father grabbed him and took him back inside, spanked him, and sent him to his room without supper.

> If you have trouble controlling your temper, it is holding you back from reaching your full potential.

In a few moments, his mother came up the stairs. She was a godly woman who often quoted the Bible to her children. As she washed his wounds and applied medicine and bandages, she began to sing songs and quote Scripture. After she applied the final bandage on his hand, she took her Bible and read from Proverbs 16:32: "Better a patient man than a warrior, a man who controls his temper than one who takes a city." Eisenhower said that he made a decision that night that he would control his anger, rather than let his anger control him. Looking back over many years, he recognized that experience as one of the turning points in his life. Because he learned to avoid rage, he became qualified to lead thousands of others.[43]

If you have trouble controlling your temper, it is holding you back from reaching your full potential. At the least, it may be keeping you from a promotion at work, and—on a much more serious level—it is likely impeding your ability to bond with your children, your spouse, and/or other loved ones. Draw the line at sinful anger once and for all. Deal with the problem before it's too late. Ask God to give you the strength and courage to respond with loving grace instead of rage, and see how He changes you from the inside out.

---

43  Wayne S. Warner, compiler, *1,000 Stories and Quotations of Famous People* (Grand Rapids, Michigan: Baker Book House, 1972), pp. 111-112.

## TO THINK ABOUT:

- Where do you see signs of our society becoming more enraged?

- When have you experienced or witnessed a rageaholic?

- Why must we be on guard against hidden, unresolved anger?

- Why is it sometimes easier to suppress our emotions than to deal with them?

- What is the balance between self-discipline and asking for God's power when it comes to handling our temper?

- What is the best way for you to control your tongue?

- How would you describe righteous anger? Have you ever experienced this type of anger? Explain.

## FOR THE FOLLOWING SCRIPTURES, ASK:
○ What does it say?    ○ What does it mean?    ○ How can you apply it?

- Proverbs 15:1
- Matthew 5:22
- Ephesians 4:26-32

# CHAPTER 12

# When You Carry More Than You Can Bear

People often attribute statements to the Bible that are not actually found in the pages of God's Word. These clever clichés have a ring of authenticity about them, which often confuses the hearer. For instance, you may have heard someone say, "The Bible says that cleanliness is next to godliness." If you search the Bible, you won't find that premise anywhere. It actually originates from a similar statement in the Jewish Talmud. While there is much to be said for cleanliness, we make a mistake to assign divine authority to such a claim.

Another common example is, "Spare the rod, spoil the child." The next time you hear it, ask the person to cite where that's found in the Bible. It isn't in God's Word. However, it sounds so "scriptural" that most people accept it as the truth. I wrote an entire book called *No, That's Not in the Bible,* about these popular but misattributed sayings.

Perhaps the most damaging misattribution people assign to the Bible is the well-intentioned statement: "God will never put more on you than you can bear." That is not in the Bible. The source of the confusion may be that this statement sounds like His promise in 1 Corinthians 10:13: "And God is faithful; he will not let you be tempted beyond what you can bear. But when you are tempted, he will also provide a way out so that you can stand up under it."

Don't miss the important distinction here. This verse speaks of temptation, not tribulation. It's true that God will never allow us to be tempted to sin beyond our ability to resist that temptation. We can't sin and complain that the temptation was too strong to resist, and the devil made us do it. However, we can't confuse that promise with the reality that Christians will sometimes face overwhelming trials.

## MORE THAN YOU CAN BEAR

Falsely believing that God won't lay more trouble on you than you can bear has caused much grief and despair for many people. When Christians crumble under the pressure of a crisis, it makes them feel as if God tricked them.

················································································

It's true that God will never allow us to be tempted to sin beyond our ability to resist that temptation.

················································································

How would the apostle Paul feel about the idea that God never puts more on people than they can bear? He would only need to point to his own life to refute that misconception. When he wrote to the church in Corinth, he recalled some of the overwhelming trials that he had already endured:

> We do not want you to be uninformed, brothers, about the hardships we suffered in the province of Asia. We were under great pressure, *far beyond our ability to endure*, so that we despaired even of life. Indeed, in our hearts we felt the sentence of death. But this happened that we might not rely on ourselves but on God, who raises the dead. He has delivered us from such a deadly peril, and he will deliver us. On him we have set our hope that he will continue to deliver us. (2 Corinthians 1:8-10, emphasis added)

In this passage, we see that God *does* sometimes put more on us than we can bear. In fact, Paul confessed that he was carrying so heavy a burden that it was beyond his human ability to endure. He fully expected to die as a result of his heavy load. Why would God allow this to happen to someone He loves? According to Paul, it happened so that he would not rely on himself but on God.

You may be going through an extremely difficult situation right now. Your hardship may be one that I addressed in this book, or it may be completely unique. Whatever it is, don't make the mistake of thinking that you can handle it on your own. It's more than you can bear because God is trying to show you that you can't carry your burden alone. Quit depending on your own feeble resources to solve your problems. Give up your efforts to resolve your difficulties. God allows you to go through trials because He wants you to rely totally on Him. He invites you to "Cast all your anxiety on him because he cares for you." (1 Peter 5:7)

Many Christians presume that it is admitting defeat to confess that they are carrying more than they can bear. They fear that something must be wrong with them or their faith. They may think they must maintain their plastic smile of contentment to protect God's reputation. You don't have to defend Him. Be honest with your emotions, and admit it when you are crushed under a burden too great for you to carry. The first step to victory is to surrender your own self-sufficiency.

...................................................................

# Be honest with your emotions, and admit it when you are crushed under a burden too great for you to carry.

...................................................................

You may hesitate to do that because you are the kind of person who has always been able to deal with your problems on your own. Your intelligence, personality, or upbringing will not be sufficient to handle life's greatest disappointments. When you encounter a problem that is beyond your capacity to solve, go ahead and admit it. It is precisely at that point when God can begin to do mighty things in your life.

## AT YOUR POINT OF DESPERATION

Life's disappointments can be God's appointments if we maintain a basic understanding of what He wants to do in our lives. God always meets us at our Point of Total Desperation. I call it being "potted" (P.O.T.D.). Are you at the P.O.T.D.? When the sun is shining and everything in our life is perfect, we tend to forget God. Some of us are so hardheaded that God allows calamity in order to get our attention.

........................................................

## When you encounter a problem that is beyond your capacity to solve, go ahead and admit it.

........................................................

Jonah is a prime example of this principle. He ran from God and ended up in the belly of a fish. It was only when he reached the P.O.T.D. that he cried out to the Lord for help. He realized that God had brought him to this point to get his attention. Jonah said, "In my distress I called to the Lord, and He answered me." (Jonah 2:2) Would Jonah have agreed if some well-intentioned person had told him that God would never lay more on him than he could bear? No way! He was beyond his ability to endure and desperate for God's help.

As long as we think we have things under control in our own strength, there is a tendency to possess a measure of pride and arrogance. We think, "Others may have problems, but I've got it all together." God allows us to carry an unbearable load at times to break us of that dangerous belief. King David paid an exorbitant price for brokenness (as we all must) because brokenness is extremely valuable. After he had committed adultery and murder by proxy, he tried to deny his guilt, but God sent Nathan the prophet to point out his folly. At one of the lowest points of his life, David prayed the words found in Psalm 51: "The sacrifices of God are a broken spirit; a broken and contrite heart, O God, you will not despise." (Psalm 51:17)

··········································································

# Have you shattered your dreams with your own hand? Treasure that brokenness and don't waste it.

··········································································

God uses disappointment to produce brokenness. Have you lost something or someone dear to you? Have you shattered your dreams with your own hand? Treasure that brokenness and don't waste it. Paul Billheimer's little book has a title that is worth the price of the book alone: *Don't Waste Your Sorrows.* God lovingly accepts a spirit of brokenness as a priceless sacrifice.

In our economy, broken things are less valuable. A broken clock is useless. A broken timing belt makes a car worthless until it can be repaired. A broken dish is usually put in the garbage. We live in a culture that discards the broken. However, in God's economy, just the opposite is true. To Him, broken things are of infinitely greater value. The clay pitchers in the hands of Gideon's army had to be broken before the light could shine out. A roof had to be broken before four friends could lower their companion to Jesus. The bread offered by the little boy had to be broken before it could be multiplied to feed 5,000. Mary's alabaster box had to be broken so she could anoint Jesus and the fragrance could fill the room. The body of Jesus had to be broken for us so that we could know the joy of salvation. While we tend to throw broken things away, God delights to use them. Cooperate with God during your difficulties,

and allow Him to produce brokenness in you. It will teach you
much more than you could learn otherwise.

> I walked a mile with laughter;
> She chatted all the way.
> But I was none the wiser;
> For all she had to say.
> I walked a mile with sorrow;
> And not a word said she.
> But, oh, the things I learned;
> When sorrow walked with me.
> –Unknown author

## WHY BAD THINGS HAPPEN TO CHRISTIANS

The Bible says we are "a chosen people, a royal priesthood, a holy
nation, a people belonging to God . . . " (1 Peter 2:9) On the
surface, it seems to be a conundrum: If God is all good (and He
is), and He is all powerful (and He is), then it would seem to make
sense that He would use His good power to prevent bad things from
happening to people—especially His people. But we know that's not
the case. Christians die in car accidents, the same as non-Christians.
Christians have cancer and heart attacks, just as atheists do.

> Cooperate with God during your
> difficulties, and allow Him to produce
> brokenness in you.

Most of us are drawn to the false assumption that if we're good,
say our prayers, and pay our taxes, then nothing bad should happen
to us or to our loved ones. There's a Seinfeld episode where Kramer
keeps saying, "Even Steven, Jerry! It all balances out!" Jerry loses a
job, then gets a phone call five minutes later offering him another

job for the same money. Jerry misses his favorite TV show, but then he catches the rerun. Elaine throws $20 of Jerry's money out the window, and Jerry finds another $20 bill wadded up in his jacket. "Even Steven, Jerry! It all balances out!"

····················································································

# I don't have to convince you that life is full of disappointments. Like Paul, we all have the scars to prove that.

····················································································

But God never promised that life would balance out. I don't have to convince you that life is full of disappointments. Like Paul, we all have the scars to prove that. Instead, I want us to consider the question, "Why?" What is the purpose behind the pain that God allows us to experience? I don't have all the answers to that question, but there are at least four reasons God allows disappointments.

### (1) To make me focus on what's really important

In 2 Corinthians 1, Paul referred to an event so painful that he fully expected to die. He wrote in verse 8, "We were under great pressure . . . so that we despaired even of life." The word Paul used for "great pressure" is the word *thlipsis*, meaning "to be crushed." We don't know exactly what hardship Paul was referring to, but he might have been referring to what happened to him in Lystra, as recorded in Acts 14, where he was almost crushed to death. Paul and Barnabas were preaching in Lystra when a mob attacked. They dragged Paul outside the city and pelted his body with jagged stones until they thought he was dead. Then they left him bleeding and unconscious beside the road. He later recovered and went back into the city.

When you're being stoned to death, I imagine that unimportant issues quickly fade away. After you get a doctor's report that you have a malignancy, you're not going to be too upset about what is going on at work. Adversity has a way of making us focus on the important things in life. Pain gets our attention. C. S. Lewis wrote two books dealing with suffering. The first was a philosophical treatise called *The Problem of Pain*. In it, he discusses pain dispassionately from an intellectual perspective. At the age of 59, Lewis married Joy Davidman Gresham, an American who was 16 years younger, divorced, a Jew, a Communist, and an atheist before she became a Christian by reading Lewis' books. When they married she had been diagnosed with cancer. She recovered for a while, and they were married for four years before she died. After her death, Lewis wrote his second book on suffering entitled, *A Grief Observed*. This second book about pain was a personal expression of his anguish over the death of his wife. Lewis wrote, "God whispers in our pleasure, but He shouts in our pain." There is nothing like suffering to narrow our focus immediately and make us keenly aware of the real issues of life and death.

### (2) To prove to me that I can't help myself

God allowed Paul to carry more than he could bear so that he would arrive at the Point of Total Desperation. We also see *why* God allowed Paul to reach that point—to teach him not to rely on his own strength. That truth debunks another biblical misquotation: "God helps those who help themselves." Wrong again. God helps the helpless. It was when Paul was going through an experience beyond his ability to endure that he learned just how helpless he was.

........................................................

## Adversity has a way of making us focus on the important things in life. Pain gets our attention.

........................................................

The Bible says in Proverbs 3:5, "Trust in the Lord with all your heart and lean not on your own understanding." You won't be able to fully trust in the Lord until you stop leaning on your own understanding and your own strength. When I was a teenager, I took lessons to become a Red Cross certified lifeguard. I remember our instructor saying that if we ever had to rescue a drowning man who was bigger and stronger than we were, we should delay reaching him until his strength was almost spent. I remember thinking that didn't make sense. Shouldn't I swim out and get him as soon as possible? Then my instructor explained that a drowning man could be dangerous because if he has the strength to fight and panic, he is liable to drown both of us. Only when he reaches the end of his strength and gives up can he safely be rescued. When we are still kicking and fighting to save ourselves, we cannot surrender to God. When we finally get to the point where we understand we have absolutely no strength left, God intervenes and rescues us.

> There are some people who say they love God, but they don't care for the Church. That's a contradiction.

Before suffering or affliction comes into your life, you may be tempted to boast, "I can handle anything!" But when you go through the pain of adversity, and reach the end of your resources, you become a much different person.

### (3) To teach me that I need the help of others

Paul gave glory to God for delivering him, but he also wrote in 2 Corinthians 1:11 how the Corinthians were helping him by their prayers. We should trust God alone to deliver us, but we need another resource as well—the help of God's people, the Church. God never intended Christians to tough it out on our own. There are some people who say they love God, but they don't care for the Church. That's a contradiction. It's like saying you love swimming, but you don't like water. Or you love to eat, but you don't like food.

The Church isn't perfect, but it's the Body of Christ on earth. It's

God's only show in town.

I'm not talking about a cold, formal, legalistic church. I'm not talking about a building on a street corner. I'm talking about God's people who love and pray for each other. Paul said, in essence, "God delivered me, but I couldn't have made it without your prayers."

The Bible says, "Carry each other's burdens, and in this way you will fulfill the law of Christ." (Galatians 6:2) The law of Christ is to love God and to love our neighbors. We love our neighbors by carrying their burdens. The Church can help you carry the burden after the death of a loved one. The Church can help you bear your burden from a devastating breakup. Other Christians can help you bear the burdens of the pains and problems we all face. We're not perfect, but we're all holding on to each other, sustaining each other.

### (4) To prepare me to help others who struggle

Paul knew the miraculous story of his deliverance would spread among the believers because he wrote in 2 Corinthians 1:11 that many people would "give thanks on our behalf for the gracious favor granted us..." He knew that his testimony would help others going through similar trials.

God has a school for His children called the University of Affliction. It has open enrollment. The tuition is rather high, and the courses are tougher than calculus or organic chemistry. The time and place of the classes are never announced in advance. You just wake up one day in the middle of your pain and discover that class has started.

····················································································

# We're not perfect, but we're all holding on to each other, sustaining each other.

····················································································

The alumni include some prominent names, including: Abraham, Moses, Hannah, David, Esther, Jeremiah, Job (he took the same class several times), Peter, Stephen, and thousands of others who suffered and survived, or suffered and died. Their struggles give strength to those of us who are now taking the same courses in the University of Affliction. Are you enrolled in God's university? You are if you are alive. Every day is a new test. And you don't graduate until you move on to heaven. You just keep taking more graduate courses. But remember, the more degrees you have, the better teacher you become.

......................................................

## God has a school for His children called the University of Affliction. It has open enrollment.

......................................................

Like you, I've been taking classes at the U of A for many years. For instance, when parents come to me concerned about a child who is suffering from severe depression, I have a little more insight to encourage them to trust God. Before I took that class, I wasn't qualified to help them. When someone comes to me with the burden of a dying parent, and the question of having to remove life support when there seems to be no hope, I have personal experience from a time when I took that same class. What are some of the painful experiences you've been through in the past? Did you lose a child? Lose a job? Lose your mate? Instead of being resentful about that tragedy, why don't you use that experience to help others who are facing the same thing?

## EVERY SCAR TELLS A STORY

When my daughters were little, they would climb into my lap and study my face. I can remember my girls pointing to a scar under my chin and asking, "Daddy, where did you get that scar?" For the fortieth time, I would tell them about how when I was a little boy, my mother came home from the hospital with my new little brother. She wasn't feeling well, and she was confined to her bed for a few days. I wanted to make her feel better, so I picked her some wildflowers growing in our garden. As I ran up our concrete steps with my bouquet, I tripped. I can remember thinking, "I can either let go of the flowers and catch myself, or I can hang onto the flowers and take it on the chin." I chose to hang onto the flowers, and the result was a visit to the doctor's office to have my chin stitched.

I received the scar on my thumb when we were building our first house, doing a lot of the work ourselves. I was putting the round sheet metal sections together for a prefab fireplace chimney one day. As I was climbing down from the roof, I fell about eight feet and my hand hit one of the sheet metal sections and almost sliced off my thumb! I have other scars, and my girls repeatedly wanted to know the stories behind all of them.

........................................................................

# Your scars should tell you the same thing so you can tell others about God's grace.

........................................................................

Think about your scars. Your scars have stories, too. It might have been a surgery, an injury, an accident, or a war wound. However, there are scars on your heart that people may never see. Despite your instinctive attempts to hide them, others desperately need to hear the story behind those scars. You should be proud of those scars because they prove that you suffered and survived. You may be divorced, but you survived. You may have lost your loved one to disease, but you are still alive to tell how God carried you through it. To paraphrase Paul, he was saying: "I have suffered, and I have scars. But I have survived, and I have a story to tell of God's deliverance." Your scars should tell you the same thing so you can tell others about God's grace. You've suffered and you will suffer again, but the same God who delivered you is the One who will deliver once more!

## TO THINK ABOUT:

- What are some other popular sayings that people mistakenly believe are in the Bible?

- Why can the belief that "God won't put more on you than you can bear" be harmful to someone spiritually and emotionally?

- When was a time that you faced something that was too big to handle on your own? What did you learn from that experience?

- Why is reaching the P.O.T.D. (Point of Total Desperation) a potential turning point in someone's life? What are the options at that moment?

- Why do you think God must sometimes use adversity to teach us life's most important lessons?

- What are you learning right now in God's University of Affliction?

## FOR THE FOLLOWING SCRIPTURES, ASK:
○ What does it say?   ○ What does it mean?   ○ How can you apply it?

- Psalm 46:1-3
- 2 Corinthians 1:8-11
- 1 Peter 5:7